REDISCOVERING FAITH

BOOKS BY THE AUTHOR

Applying the Kingdom

God's Big Idea

In Pursuit of Purpose

Kingdom Parenting

Kingdom Principles

Myles Munroe 365-Day Devotional

The Glory of Living

The Purpose and Power of Love & Marriage

The Purpose and Power of Praise & Worship

Rediscovering the Kingdom

Releasing Your Potential

Single, Married, Separated and Life After Divorce

Understanding Your Potential

Waiting and Dating

AVAILABLE FROM DESTINY IMAGE PUBLISHERS

REDISCOVERING FAITH

UNDERSTANDING THE NATURE OF KINGDOM LIVING

MYLES MUNROE

DESTINY IMAGE® PUBLISHERS, INC.
P.O. Box 310, Shippensburg, PA 17257-0310

"Speaking to the Purposes of God for This Generation and for the Generations to Come."

Bahamas Faith Ministry
PO Box N9583
Nassau, Bahamas

This book and all other Destiny Image, Revival Press, MercyPlace, Fresh Bread, Destiny Image Fiction, and Treasure House books are available at Christian bookstores and distributors worldwide.

For a U.S. bookstore nearest you, call **1-800-722-6774.**

For more information on foreign distributors, call **717-532-3040.**

Or reach us on the Internet: **www.destinyimage.com.**

HARDCOVER:
ISBN 10: 0-7684-3092-5
ISBN 13: 978-0-7684-3092-9

PAPERBACK:
ISBN 10: 0-7684-3137-9
ISBN 13: 978-0-7684-3137-7

For Worldwide Distribution, Printed in the U.S.A.

Hardcover   1 2 3 4 5 6 7 8 9 10 11 / 13 12 11 10 09
Trade Paper 1 2 3 4 5 6 7 8 9 10 11 / 13 12 11 10 09

DEDICATION

To my beloved wife of over 30 years, Ruth, and my precious children, Charisa and Chairo Myles Jr. Your faith in my leadership of our family taught me the greatest lesson of faith in my heavenly Father.

To my beloved father and dad, Matthias Munroe, whose steadfast faith in God through the many trials and challenges of raising eleven respectable and successful children inspired me to believe that nothing is impossible.

To my sister Suzan Hall and her late husband Steve: Your commitment to God and the display of an exceptional quality of faith in the face of sickness and even death gives me the impetus to face my future with stainless confidence.

To the millions of people of the Third World nations who struggle daily with the twists and turns of an unpredictable life: May this book become a source of encouragement and fuel your faith to believe in a better tomorrow.

To the author and finisher of my faith, Jesus Christ: Thank You for having faith in me enough to die to restore my faith in You.

ACKNOWLEDGMENTS

No form of accomplishment in life is ever the result of individual isolated effort, but the product of the contribution and corporate support of many people in our lives. This work is no different. I want to thank my close friend and editor over the years, Don Milam, who continues to encourage me to put my thoughts in print believing that they can help others on this earthly journey. Don, your contribution and follow-up on this project made it possible for me to deliver this manuscript to the world.

Thanks also to my wife, Ruth, and children, Charisa and Chairo, who continue to allow me to spend nights and days buried in the pages of research and staring at the screen of my laptop in order to produce this work. Thank you, and I love you all.

To Sandra Kemp, a woman with so much faith that she refuses to lie down and die, but continues the good fight of faith never doubting the faithfulness of her God to deliver her from the pain of physical discomfort. Thanks for the inspiration.

The members of Bahamas Faith Ministries Fellowship on Nassau, Bahamas, whose faith in me as your leader forced me to seek answers to questions and issues that needed addressing. This book is the result of one of those searches. Thank you.

CONTENTS

Preface 11

Prologue 15

Introduction 19

Chapter One   Where Is Your Faith? 23

Chapter Two   Faith: The Culture of the Kingdom 51

Chapter Three   Kingdom Faith Is Tested Faith 75

Chapter Four   The Ten Qualities of Kingdom Faith 95

Chapter Five   Let God Be God 115

Chapter Six   The Courage of Kingdom Faith 133

Chapter Seven   Faith Beyond the Test, Part 1 155

Chapter Eight   Faith Beyond the Test, Part 2 175

Chapter Nine   The Power of Kingdom Faith 193

Chapter Ten   Faith That Overcomes the World 211

Conclusion 229

PREFACE

No man can live beyond his belief! The greatest loss in life is the loss of belief! The greatest challenge in life is to believe in the midst of life itself. The greatest challenge of daily life is that life is too daily. Life never stops!

Have you ever wished that the earth would stop spinning and let you off for a while to take a break from its nonstop mire of demands, decisions, attentions, questions, challenges, responsibilities, expectations, promises, and obligations? Do you feel the pressure of the expected demands of daily life? Bills to pay, job to keep, children to raise, spouse to support, house to secure and protect, food to eat, water to drink, clothes to wear, friends to manage, taxes to pay, and a reputation to maintain?

Then there is the unexpected! The loss of a job, the death of a parent or spouse or child, the discovery of a terminal sickness in your family or your own body, the termination of a friendship or a marital divorce, the oppression of a personal habit or the abuse of substances by a family member, or the failure of your business venture. This is life on planet Earth. All earth dwellers must face the same challenges, and whether you succeed or fail will be determined by how you manage the predictable and the unpredictable.

Most of our fellow planet dwellers are experiencing hardship, frustration, depression, and ultimate failure in their bid to face these challenges. Many prefer to pretend the challenges don't exist while others drown their inability to cope in a sea of alcohol, drugs, and other self-destructive, antisocial behaviors. Many have lost confidence in the political, social, economic, and religious systems of their nations and have opted out of mainstream life. Many no longer think there can be peace on earth or accept that the United Nations can prevent wars. Others have given up on politicians to solve our national problems or scientists to meet our medical and environmental challenges. Still others live in daily fear of terrorism or helplessly stand by and watch the devaluation of human life through ethnic cleansing, abortions, or war campaigns. Humanity has been led to a critical crossroad! Humanity is now wondering if there is an alternative to our world as we have made it. In essence, most of humanity has simply stopped believing. They have lost faith in faith.

It is an absolute tragedy to lose a job, a spouse, a child, a home, or a business, but these are not the greatest losses one can experience. The greatest loss in life on earth is the loss of belief. *When one loses belief, one loses hope!* When hope is lost, then purpose is cancelled, and meaning has no definition. Belief is the source of reason and the raw material for commitment, persistence, and faithfulness. When belief is lost, then life has no explanation. No matter what you might lose in the midst of daily life never lose your faith in life.

This book is about this very challenge! It's about the need not just for faith, but for the right kind of faith. Much of what we call faith today is simply convenient expectation! In other words, we only believe what we want, expect, and are willing to accept. Our belief is based on what we define and interpret as good, right, and acceptable; and therefore, instead of believing in the sovereign nature and omniscient perspective of the Creator, our faith is only valid as long as our experiences are in keeping with our definition of good.

This book is written to challenge the quality and nature of the faith you have inherited from our contemporary belief systems and to test them against the record of the time-tested champions of a faith that overcame every type of challenge in their time.

My intent is to cause you to question the kind of faith you have embraced and to see whether it is of the quality that can stand the test of disappointments—the unexpected crisis moments filled with the silence of God and the loss of everything you hold dear. What kind of faith do you have? Can you believe in the dark what you were told in the light? Can you still believe in something after losing everything? Can you believe in hope even when hope stops believing in you? When in doubt can you have faith?

My hope is that these pages will ignite the kind of belief in you that will propel you through life and position you with a faith that threatens tragedy and becomes a crisis to crisis. It is my desire that you rediscover the faith of the lost culture of the Kingdom of Heaven and begin living at a level of life that does not get bogged down in the constant changes of life on earth. The goal of this book is to help us all restore the power of Kingdom Faith.

PROLOGUE

The 2008 global economic crisis which began with the collapse of major financial institutions in the United States then rippled throughout Europe, the Asian Pacific, Africa, South America, the Far East, and even my region of the Caribbean exposed a number of vital and important components that make nations function effectively: (1) the interdependence of nations, economies, and societies; (2) the critical role of currency value in the functioning of the economy. The truth is all countries and social societies must develop and maintain a currency of exchange that allows for trading, exchange of goods, and transaction of business within the social system. This economy of currency is established by the governing authority of the nation and serves as the sustaining component of everyday functioning and stability of the nation. Without this common national currency it would be impossible to exist as a nation. Nothing happens without currency, and so everyone in the social structure pursues access to and possession of this currency.

The Kingdom of Heaven is also a country, though an invisible one, and as such also functions on a currency of trade and transaction. The Kingdom of Heaven's culture is Love; its atmosphere is Hope; and its common currency is Faith. The currency of the Kingdom of Heaven is Faith. The vital necessity, priority, and value of Faith for life in the Kingdom of Heaven on earth are underscored by the statements made about its role in the Kingdom by the King Himself. Without faith, the Kingdom cannot function. Note the following:

> …*According to your faith will it be done to you…* (Matthew 9:29-30).

> *And He did not do many miracles there because of their lack of faith…* (Matthew 13:58).

> …*Woman, you have great faith! Your request is granted…* (Matthew 15:28).

> *He replied, "Because you have so little faith. I tell you the truth, if you have faith as small as a mustard seed, you can say to this mountain, 'Move from here to there' and it will move. Nothing will be impossible for you"* (Matthew 17:20).

> *Jesus replied, "I tell you the truth, if you have faith and do not doubt, not only can you do what was done to the fig tree, but also you can say to this mountain, 'Go, throw yourself into the sea,' and it will be done. If you believe, you will receive whatever you ask for in prayer"* (Matthew 21:21-22).

> *When Jesus saw their faith, He said to the paralytic, "Son, your sins are forgiven"* (Mark 2:5).

And He was amazed at their lack of faith (Mark 6:6).

*I tell you, He will see that they get justice, and quickly.
However, when the Son of Man comes, will He find
faith on the earth? (Luke 18:8).*

*…We have been saying that Abraham's faith was
credited to him as righteousness (Romans 4:9).*

Therefore, the promise comes by faith…
(Romans 4:16).

*And without faith it is impossible to please God,
because anyone who comes to Him must believe that
He exists and that He rewards those who earnestly
seek Him (Hebrews 11:6).*

*For therein is the righteousness of God revealed from
faith to faith: as it is written, The just shall live by faith*
(Romans 1:17 KJV).

*Now the just shall live by faith: but if any man draw
back, My soul shall have no pleasure in him*
(Hebrews 10:38 KJV).

These statements clearly indicate the necessity of faith for functioning in the economy and society of the Kingdom of Heaven on
earth. The essence of this Kingdom currency is that nothing in the
Kingdom can be experienced or appropriated without "believing"
it is truth and "expecting" it is your right as a citizen to receive. The
Kingdom is activated by believing it is real, relevant, and present. We

must believe the Kingdom government and its constitutional promises, having full conviction that it will function in your life now and in the future.

"Have faith in God," Jesus answered (Mark 11:22).

May your account be filled with an abundant deposit of faith, and may you benefit from investing it in your daily life.

INTRODUCTION

"When in doubt…have faith."

The wheels of our massive 747 jet plane kissed the hot Egyptian airport runway with a thud after 15 hours of flying, recording another smooth landing in my now normal world travels. It was my first trip to Cairo. The desert heat of this ancient city greeted my wife and I like a hot blanket, and immediately I felt I had just walked through a time warp into history. All the stories I had read and learned from a child about this far-removed country suddenly exploded in my mind, and now the land had become a living specimen stretched out before me like an Indiana Jones adventure.

I have traveled thousands of miles to over 70 nations and experienced a myriad of cities, cultures, climates, and social and religious customs, yet each new place rekindles a childlike spirit of anticipation like an unknown mystery novel beckoning me to explore its unread pages. Cairo was such a city. The biblical writings of the great leader and deliverer, Moses, in his five books of the Old Testament, left us an historical record filled with events that took place in this land rich with culture. We stayed for seven days and traveled throughout the land visiting the ancient cities of Cairo, Luxor, and the world-famous ancient tombs of the Egyptian pharaohs, the pyramids.

I could recall the overwhelming feeling I had walking through the ancient ruins of Luxor, straining my neck to view the colossal pillars from the temple and the massive carvings and hieroglyphics beautifully preserved as if they were written yesterday. As I surveyed the evidence of a civilization that still baffles the modern mind, I could not help but feel the power of the mystery of the unknown. So many questions filled my mind! How were these magnificent edifices built? How did they transport and lift the massive stones that towered over our tiny human frames? What kind of rituals of events took place in these hallowed halls? What were these people like, and what were their motivations?

My unanswered questions were further magnified the next day when we arrived at the long-anticipated pyramids. From the pages of many history books I had as a child, I had imagined what they must have looked like, but my imagination could not prepare me for what I saw that day. There under the sweltering heat of the desert sun stood before me what millions dream of seeing, the three major pyramids of the ancient Egyptian kings and pharaohs. As our guide led us to the first structure, suddenly I felt myself shrink as if in a miniature world. I was awestruck first by the literal size of the stones that composed the structure—each being larger than any car or bus I had seen. Then there was the massive height of the actual structure, coupled with the perfect angles that stretched up toward the cloudless sky.

My imagination was again assailed when we actually entered the opening that led into the inner cells of this once-sacred burial place of the mighty leaders of Egypt. I could feel the civilizations flowing over my life as we surveyed an elegant display of the remains of the boy-pharaoh, King Tut. There in glass cases in this large, spacious room were artifacts of the splendor of ancient Egypt. I must confess I was completely overwhelmed as was my wife and many others who stood by.

Questions flooded my mind like a tidal wave. The trip ended that day the way it had begun—with more questions than answers—and with the conclusion that the reality of life is found in its mysteries. You will never have all the answers! You will never know everything! You will never solve every problem. You will never resolve all dilemmas. There will always be things in life you cannot explain. Sometimes living life without explanations is a challenge we must accept. It is the blank spaces in life's experiences that cause great bewilderment. There are some things we will never understand. What do you do when you don't know what to do? You have to still believe. The mysteries of life will always make room for faith.

CHAPTER ONE

WHERE IS YOUR FAITH?

"Faith makes all things possible…love makes all things easy."

Life is full of mysteries. Questions on the nature and meaning of life are universal in every culture and in every generation. Everyone ponders the purpose of life to one degree or another. Like our ancestors before us we stare into the starlit night sky in awed wonderment at the majesty of the heavens and ask, "Where did I come from? Why am I here?" We share a common bond with the psalmist of old who wrote: *"When I consider Your heavens, the work of Your fingers, the moon and the stars, which You have set in place, what is man that You are mindful of him, the son of man that You care for him?"* (Ps. 8:3-4). We gaze into the face of a newborn baby and marvel at the mystery and magnificence of new life. Large or small, mystery fills our day-to-day existence. Another ancient writer expressed it well: *"There are three things that are too amazing for me, four that I do not understand: the way of an eagle in the sky, the way of a snake on a rock, the way of a ship on the high seas, and the way of a man with a maiden"* (Prov. 30:18-19). Mystery surrounds us. Mystery is part of what makes life worth living.

Many people don't see it that way, however. They want life broken into bite-size pieces for easy consumption. Uncomfortable with mystery, they want the meaning of life distilled into diagrams and bullet points with no confusion, no uncertainty, and nothing left to chance. Unfortunately, they are bound to be disappointed because life simply isn't like that.

If we want to build fulfilled and stable lives of purpose and meaning, we must be willing to embrace mystery. We must accept the fact that we will never know everything we would like to know. Some things will always be out of our reach, some issues perpetually beyond our understanding. This means we must approach life with a healthy dose of humility and admit that we do not—and cannot—know it all. Our attitude must be like that of David, the poet-king of ancient Israel, who wrote, *"My heart is not proud, O Lord, my eyes are not haughty; I do not concern myself with great matters or things too wonderful for me. But I have stilled and quieted my soul; like a weaned child with its mother, like a weaned child is my soul within me. O Israel, put your hope in the Lord both now and forevermore"* (Ps. 131:1-3). Humility and faith will help us deal with the mysteries of life.

The Mysteries of Life

What do you do when life hits you on the blind side? How do you react when the unexpected happens? Imagine what you would think if your newly married spouse dies. Your father takes his life. Your mother turns out not to be your biological mother of 30 years. Your sister is a prostitute. Your father reveals his secret homosexual lifestyle. Your new house burns down. Your healthy child suddenly dies, or your first pregnancy ends in stillbirth. Your total life's savings and investment in a company or institution is lost. Your family members die in a plane crash leaving infants to care for. How do you ever explain or understand these tragedies?

There are questions in life we can never answer. Some people insist on knowing the answers to everything. They assume that no area of knowledge is beyond human understanding. Consequently, when something stumps them, they become depressed. Our insatiable pursuit of knowledge and understanding is perfectly natural—to a point. After all, our Creator designed us to be curious about ourselves and the world we live in. The key is to keep everything in proper perspective. Part of that perspective is acknowledging that there are some things we simply will never understand.

People sometimes ask me why I never seem to be depressed or frustrated. One reason is because I realized 30 years ago that there are some questions I will never be able to answer. I search out whatever answers I can, accept the fact that some things elude me (and probably always will), and move on. There are some questions we will never be able to answer. Acknowledging this truth makes life so much easier.

There are things in life we can never explain. Some things we see or experience in life defy rational explanation. Just accept them. You will enjoy life more. Psychiatric wards are full of people who cracked under the strain of trying to explain the unexplainable. Settle in your mind now that there are some things you will never be able to explain. Otherwise, you will be depressed all the time.

There are things in life we can never change. Today I enjoy life no matter what happens because 30 years ago I realized that there are some things that I cannot change, so it is useless to try. It's been said that 90 percent of life consists of things we cannot change. Most of us live frustrated lives because we spend all our time fretting and worrying about the 90 percent of life we cannot change instead of focusing on the 10 percent we *can* change. Weeping, worrying, and wailing about the unfairness of life will change nothing except, perhaps, your blood pressure, so don't fall into that trap.

There are things in life we cannot control. Some people are obsessed with control; they have to micromanage every aspect of life, not only for themselves, but also for everyone around them. We all know someone like this: a boss, a parent, a child, a spouse. Most of us have witnessed or experienced the devastating effect a domineering personality can have on the lives of others.

Ultimately, however, none of us can control what anyone else does, not even those closest to us. We can teach them our values, make known our wishes, and even "lay down the law," but in the end they make their own choices and bear responsibility for those choices. And we do the same. Maybe your spouse has decided to leave you. You can beg, bargain, cry, cajole, and even pray, but if he or she is determined to leave, there is nothing you can do. Perhaps a sibling or a son or daughter is abusing drugs. You can rant, rave, preach, and pester, but you really have little control over the choices he or she makes. Let's face it; there are some things in life we cannot control, no matter how much we wish it were otherwise. Accept this fact.

There are things in life we cannot stop. If you are standing on a railroad track with a train coming toward you at full speed, you have two choices: get out of the way or get run over. Life is like that sometimes. Some things that come at you are unstoppable, so you must learn how to make arrangements for them to pass you by. If you try to stand in the way and stop it like a person facing down a speeding train with his hand raised, it will continue on to where it is going, and you will be destroyed in the process.

There are things in life for which we are not responsible. No matter how well we raise our children, they still may make unwise decisions or foolish mistakes that carry severe consequences. No matter how carefully we prepare for the contingencies of life—finances, health,

retirement, etc.—adversity may come from a completely unexpected quarter and knock it down. Sometimes we do our best and
bad things still happen. We are not responsible for those things. We
are responsible only for how we *respond* to those things and for what
we do with the time and resources we have.

There are things in life we cannot exceed. Some people don't know
their limits, while others refuse to accept any limitations. Such an
attitude is both arrogant and foolish. All of us have limits, and we
will be much happier when we acknowledge those limits. One of my
favorite statements in life that has kept me at peace is: "I don't know."
That is one of the most powerful and empowering statements any of
us can make in life.

A prayer written many years ago by American pastor and theo-
logian Reinhold Niebuhr captures perfectly the attitude we should
take toward the mysteries of life. The first part of the prayer is very
familiar to most of us, but the second part is just as apropos:

> God grant me the serenity to accept the things I cannot
> change; courage to change the things I can; and wisdom to
> know the difference.
> Living one day at a time;
> Enjoying one moment at a time;
> Accepting hardships as the pathway to peace;
> Taking, as He did, this sinful world
> as it is, not as I would have it;
> Trusting that He will make all things right
> if I surrender to His will;
> That I may be reasonably happy in this life
> and supremely happy with Him
> Forever in the next.
> Amen.[1]

Facing Life Successfully

With so much mystery and uncertainty in life, how can we have any hope of facing life with confidence? How can we be assured of success in life when so much is hidden from us? The secret of success is *knowledge*. This is just as true for life as for any other endeavor. The key to successful living lies in knowing four things.

First, *we must know our limitations*. The Bible says that if we believe we are more than we are, then we lack wisdom and are worse off than a foolish person: *"Do you see a man wise in his own eyes? There is more hope for a fool than for him"* (Prov. 26:12). The original Hebrew word for *fool* here literally means "stupid" or "silly." In other words, the stupidest people in the world are those who think too highly of themselves. Everyone has limitations, and if we are wise, we will recognize our own. We have to know where the line is drawn, where we have to stop. We must know when we have gone as far as we can go.

God never expects us to move beyond our limitations *on our own*. Anything He asks of us, however, He will empower us to accomplish, even if it seems impossible from our vantage point. *We* have limitations, but God does not: *"For nothing is impossible with God"* (Luke 1:37). Knowing our limitations frees us to walk and live in God's infinite capability. Only then can we "do the impossible" as we tap into His limitlessness.

Second, *we must know what we are responsible for*. For example, we are each responsible for the decisions we make every day. Many people today like to play the "blame game" by refusing to accept responsibility for their own choices and actions. Instead, they claim to be victims of their environment, their upbringing, or the behavior of other people. This game is as old as Eden, where Adam and Eve blamed each other for their own disobedience to God. In all honesty, we cannot blame anyone but ourselves for the decisions we make and the consequences they bring. Not only are we responsible for our decisions, we are responsible also for how we *respond* to the adversities that life sometimes throws our way. We often have little control over what happens to us, but we do control the way adversity affects our lives, and that is where our responsibility lies.

Third, *we must know what we are* not *responsible for.* This is just as important as the previous point. Just as we are responsible for some things, we are not responsible for other things. For example, although we bear responsibility for our own actions, we are not responsible for the actions of others. Our free will is under our control, but the free will of others is not. Even God Himself is not responsible for our free will. He will do everything He can to influence our choices, but He will not make those choices for us. Jesus Christ died on the cross for us. He freely gave His life for us, shedding His blood so that we could be forgiven of our sins and become eternal citizens of the Kingdom of His Father. Then He rose from the dead as a guarantee that all who turn to Him will receive eternal life. Jesus did all of this—yet He still cannot save us without our permission. He knows His limitation; it is self-imposed. Violating our free will is a line He will not cross. There are some things we are not responsible for, and successful living means knowing where those boundaries are.

Fourth, *we must know what we cannot do.* Basically, this sums up the other three. Success in life means learning not to walk in guilt over circumstances or consequences that are beyond our control. Many parents waste year after year blaming themselves for the foolish decisions of their adult children. And how many of us get caught up in the "if onlys" of regret, often over matters we could not have changed then any more than we could change them now. That's no way to live. We cannot keep blaming ourselves for things we cannot change. Contentment and success in life come when we acknowledge that there are some things we cannot do. *Our greatest point of weakness is when we arrive at the wall of our limitation.*

What's Your Motive?

Once we acknowledge the mysteries and unknowns of life and accept the fact of our own limitations, what are we left with? How do we live successfully under such conditions? There is only one way: faith. *It is my conviction that mankind was created and designed to live by this essential principle called faith. It is belief in the unseen and hope for the unknown that energizes the human spirit.* Our Creator, the King of the universe, is looking for strong faith on the part of the people He created in His own image. Whenever He finds it, He strengthens it even more: *"For the eyes of the Lord range throughout the earth to strengthen those whose hearts are fully committed to Him"* (2 Chron. 16:9a). At one point, Jesus Himself asked, *"When the Son of Man comes, will He find faith on the earth?"* (Luke 18:8b). God is looking for strong faith. *It is interesting to note that He did not expect to find power, authority, wealth, influence, religion, politics, commerce, education, or traditions, but faith. Perhaps He sees faith as the most important component on planet Earth.*

Your faith is only as strong as the tests it survives. How strong are you? Strength must be tested before it can be considered reliable. You are only as strong as what you can lift, so never brag about your own strength unless you have tested it first.

On one of my many trips around the world, I sat next to a middle-aged gentleman on the plane. After settling in for the 11-hour flight to London, I asked him what he did as a profession. He said. "I am a test driver and pilot." I was immediately intrigued and dove into an enlightening conversation that became a college course in the art and science of machine testing. He proceeded to educate me on the purposes, preparations, skills, and thrills involved in his work. Then I asked him the big question: "Why is it necessary to test a new car or aircraft engine?" His answer changed my life! He stated that every credible manufacturer invests in testing their products in order to guarantee its performance and to verify their claims regarding the product. He said testing was necessary to establish the measure of trust you can promise the customer. In essence, testing is a prerequisite for trust. Simply put, *tests verify claims*.

Many believers walk around daily making claims and praising and worshiping God—testifying to how good He is and how much He has blessed them—but their faith has never truly been tested. It is easy to say, "God is good" when things are going well, but what about the bad times? What about the times when you can't pay your rent or your light bill, or when you lose your job? Under those circumstances can you still say, "God is good"? Just as He did with Job, God allows our faith to be tested so we can see how strong we are. God had blessed Job greatly, yet He allowed satan to strip Job of everything he had—family, wealth, health—to see whether Job's faith would stand the test. If you say, "I believe God," get ready, because God will allow the testing of your belief so that you and others will see whether or not it is true. His purpose is not to humiliate you or to catch you in a lie, but to help you grow because He knows that untested faith is not valid faith and never amounts to much.

The testing of our faith serves not only to show the strength of our faith but also to reveal the *motive* behind our faith. If you say, "I trust in God," *why* do you trust in God? Is it because of who He is or because of what you hope to get out of it? Satan accused Job of following God only because God had blessed him, so God allowed Job to be tested. He wanted to reveal the motive behind Job's faith, to reveal whether or not Job would continue to follow God even after he lost everything. *In the Kingdom of God, as in any country, your belief in the nation's constitutional promises and privileges can only be verified when circumstances require that you place a demand on the system. The testing of your faith in the Kingdom of God occurs through circumstances which provide an opportunity for you to validate your belief in the political, economic, social, and cultural system of Heaven on earth.*

The Power of Motive and Faith

Have you ever watched a report on a tragic murder or horrific incident and wondered why the first major question asked by the authorities would be "what was the motive?" This is because the most powerful force for human behavior is motive! Everything we do is generated by some motive. What is motive? Motive is the hidden reason or desire that initiates, sustains, and justifies an action. All human action, no matter what we claim to the contrary, is a product of a motive. Motive is internally justified reason. As a matter of fact, the absence of motive is a sign of death. Life itself depends on motivation to give it meaning. Where there is no motivation, there is no passion or energy. We all do everything for a reason. It is motive that moves us. We are victims of our motives, and we protect them from exposure.

Why is motive so important to the subject of faith? Motive is birthed by our beliefs and convictions.

What is your motive for following God? The answer to that question lies at the very heart of life. What motivated you to acknowledge Jesus Christ as your Lord and to enter His Kingdom? These are important questions because they test the motive of your faith. The sixth chapter of John's Gospel opens with an account of Jesus feeding a crowd of 5,000 people with only five loaves of bread and two fish. Afterward He retreated into the hills to be alone while His disciples sailed their boat to the other side of the Sea of Galilee. Later that night He joined them in the boat by walking to them on the water. The next day, the crowd who had been fed so miraculously the day before went looking for Jesus but could not find Him.

> *Once the crowd realized that neither Jesus nor His disciples were there, they got into the boats and went to Capernaum in search of Jesus.*
>
> *When they found Him on the other side of the lake, they asked Him, "Rabbi, when did You get here?"*
>
> *Jesus answered, "I tell you the truth, you are looking for Me, not because you saw miraculous signs but because you ate the loaves and had your fill. Do not work for food that spoils, but for food that endures to eternal life, which the Son of Man will give you. On Him God the Father has placed His seal of approval* (John 6:24-27).

The people were looking for Jesus not because of who He was but for what He could do for them. He could feed them; He could heal their bodies; He could cast demons out of their lives. Their motives were self-serving, and Jesus knew it. He told them, in effect, "*I know why you're here. You aren't looking for Me; you're looking for a blessing. You're looking for more free fish and bread.*" Your motive conceals and reveals the quality and nature of your faith.

Don't we love it when God blesses us? And He has promised to bless us. He has promised to add things to us. But blessings should not be our motive for following Jesus. What if He doesn't bless today? What if He doesn't add anything today? What then? Do we turn away and go somewhere else? Or do we continue to follow Jesus even when we're not being blessed? What's our motive? *This is the question of Kingdom faith: "Can you follow the light even in the dark?"*

Jesus said, *"Do not work for food that spoils, but for food that endures to eternal life, which the Son of Man will give you."* In other words, we should not waste our faith on things that can go away in the morning. Instead, we should place our trust in the "Son of Man," upon whom "God the Father has placed His seal of approval." The only thing in life that is sealed and secure is Christ. He is the only trustworthy and reliable object of our faith—not His blessings, His provision, or His healings, but Jesus Christ Himself. *Even the blessings of God are temporary, and thus we should place no faith in them.*

Faith in Christ: the Work of God

Like the crowd that sought out Jesus in Capernaum so long ago, many people today follow Him only for His blessings. You may trust in God because He heals people, but will you still trust Him when He doesn't heal someone and that person dies? You trust God to provide your rent money, but will you still trust Him when the rent is due and the money is not there? You trust God to protect your children, but will you still trust Him when one of them starts doing drugs or gets in trouble with the law? Where is your faith? Is it in Christ or in what He can do for you? *In the Kingdom of God our faith is more in the nature of God than the products of God.*

Jesus' response to the crowd that day must have ruffled their feathers because they followed up with some challenging questions:

> Then they asked Him, *"What must we do to do the works God requires?"*

Jesus answered, "The work of God is this: to believe in the One He has sent."

So they asked Him, "What miraculous sign then will you give that we may see it and believe you? What will you do? Our forefathers ate the manna in the desert; as it is written: 'He gave them bread from heaven to eat.'"

Jesus said to them, "I tell you the truth, it is not Moses who has given you the bread from heaven, but it is My Father who gives you the true bread from heaven. For the bread of God is He who comes down from heaven and gives life to the world" (John 6:28-33).

The people were confused. In essence they said to Jesus, "Well, if we are not supposed to follow You for bread or fish or anything else we can get from You, then what are we supposed to do?"

"Simple," Jesus replied. "Believe on the One the Father sent." In other words, don't believe on the bread, don't believe on the fish, don't believe on the miracles. *Don't put your faith in the activities of God because He may not act in the way you expect.* This does not mean He is unfaithful or untrustworthy. It simply means that His purpose and will are not always completely visible from our limited vantage point. God's purpose is always greater than any of our personal perspectives or circumstances. *This is one reason why He calls us to trust in Him and not His works.* He is shifting our motivation from *things to Him and His nature* because things change. Things deteriorate. Things rust and break and fade away and are consumed. Things are temporary and therefore unworthy of our trust. Only *God Jehovah and His Christ are* eternal, and only that which is placed in His care will last.

The people around Jesus that day tried to compare their experience with bread and fish to the experience of the Israelites in the desert, when manna (bread) came down from Heaven to feed them. Apparently they were trying to convince Jesus that they followed Moses because of the miracles: manna, liberation from Egyptian slavery, the parting of the Red Sea. Jesus countered by reminding them that the manna did not come from Moses but from God. It is dangerous to trust in miracles because miracles are temporary. The mortgage payment is temporary. The car payment is temporary. We never know what God is thinking unless He chooses to reveal His thoughts. He can provide the mortgage payment or car payment, or He can test us to see if we can still be at peace in Him even if we miss a payment.

This is why Jesus tells us to *put our faith not in the things of God but in the God of the things.* He says, "It is My Father who gives you the true bread from heaven. For the bread of God is He who comes down from heaven and gives life to the world." There are two kinds of bread being discussed here. First is the "bread" of blessings, such as manna or the bread the people ate that Jesus provided. The second kind of bread is the "true bread" or "bread of God" that came down from Heaven. Both the bread of blessing and the true bread come from the same place—Heaven—but the bread of blessing is temporary. We are not supposed to become satisfied with it. The purpose of the bread of blessing is to whet our appetite for the true bread. And what is the nature of the true bread? *The principle of this discourse with the people is to teach us that the Source is always more important than the resource and the Manufacturer more important than the product. This is critical because the resource is dispensable, but the Source is permanent. We should never put our faith in the resource but in the Source.* Jesus explains,

> *"Sir," they said, "from now on give us this bread."*
> *Then Jesus declared, "I am the bread of life. He who*
> *comes to Me will never go hungry, and he who believes*
> *in Me will never be thirsty. But as I told you, you have*
> *seen Me and still you do not believe"* (John 6:34-36).

In the Kingdom of God the issue is not how much faith you have, but *where your faith is placed.* Are you following Jesus Christ, or are you following signs and wonders and prosperity? Is your faith in Jesus Christ the "bread of life," or are you satisfied with the bread of blessing? Are you seeking to satisfy your spirit or merely trying to fill your belly? Are you trusting in things that never truly satisfy or in the One who satisfies forever? *Most people I have met focus their faith on the bread and not the Baker. The principle of Kingdom faith is to trust the Source and not the resource.*

Make no mistake about it: the Kingdom of God will meet our every need, absolutely. But it is for this very reason that we are not to trust in those things that will meet our needs but in the King who provides them. As Kingdom citizens, our business is to trust, obey, and serve the King; His business is to take care of us. This is what Jesus meant when He said,

> *So do not worry, saying, "What shall we eat?" or "What*
> *shall we drink?" or "What shall we wear?" For the*
> *pagans run after all these things, and your heavenly*
> *Father knows that you need them. But seek first His*
> *kingdom and His righteousness, and all these things*
> *will be given to you as well* (Matthew 6:31-33).

We don't follow God for what we can get from Him. Kingdom faith is faith in the King, not the King's favor. It is faith in Him, not His gifts.

REDISCOVERING FAITH

Faith in the Midst of Hardship

Living in the beautiful islands of the Bahamas in the Caribbean all my life, I have enjoyed the pleasure of the crystal clear ocean, abundant sea food, the perfect annual average temperature of 75 degrees, the economic and political stability that makes our nation the envy of many, and the warm spirit of our people that drew over five million tourists to our shores for years. Yet this island paradise where life is like a dream every day is also in the path of the annual hurricane or cyclone track. During my life in these beautiful islands, we have had to endure many major hurricanes that test not only the durability of nature, structures, and people, but most importantly, the trust we have in our governing system to guide and protect us through these horrific storms. Even so, Kingdom faith is designed not just for good times, but also for difficult times. I remember as a child and even today as an adult, our family gathering together, riveted to the radio, listening to minute-by-minute reports of the storms provided by the government national Radio Broadcasting Corporation. As the 130 mph winds howled and the trees fell all around us, our roof would shake, and the crash of thunder and lightning would make us wonder if we would survive.

Our entire confidence was in the government's agencies and their building codes which were warranted to protect us and ensure our survival. The government building codes of our country were determined by our location in the hurricane and whether we obeyed the code, building our foundation and structure in accordance with it; if so, then the government guaranteed the houses would stand the test of any storm. I am pleased to report at the writing of this manuscript that we have never had a house structure collapse on us during a major storm. In essence, the government codes build the nation for the inevitable tests. Our obedience to the codes brings us peace and confidence in the storms and minimizes fear.

The spiritual-supernatural country of the Kingdom of Heaven with its established colony on earth is no different. The heavenly government and its constitutional promises guarantee the security of its citizens and establish building codes for the community of the Kingdom which are designed for the storms of life. Many Kingdom citizens assume that if they are going through difficult times, it means they do not have enough faith. Not so. Kingdom faith does not remove us from hardship; it preserves and protects us through hardship. Once again, the key is where we place our faith not how much faith we have. On one occasion the King of Heaven addressed this very issue of faith in the building code of His Kingdom:

> *Therefore everyone who hears these words of mine and puts them into practice is like a wise man who built his house on the rock. The rain came down, the streams rose, and the winds blew and beat against that house; yet it did not fall, because it had its foundation on the rock. But everyone who hears these words of mine and does not put them into practice is like a foolish man who built his house on sand. The rain came down, the streams rose, and the winds blew and beat against that house, and it fell with a great crash* (Matthew 7:24-27).

The concept of tests, trials, and storms in the life of the Kingdom citizen on earth is not one that should be foreign and unexpected but rather anticipated with confidence and faith. Kingdom faith embraces storms and proves its worth in trials. The King of the Kingdom in relating this concept said to His citizens on another occasion:

> *I have told you these things, so that in Me you may*
> *have peace. In this world you will have trouble. But*
> *take heart! I have overcome the world* (John 16:33).

Another governmental promise assures the Kingdom citizen,

> *I have given you authority to trample on snakes and*
> *scorpions and to overcome all the power of the enemy;*
> *nothing will harm you* (Luke 10:19).

Has anyone ever asked you, "Well, if God is so good, why is this happening to you?" Jesus answers that question right here. Perhaps you have questioned why you are facing difficult challenges or wondered if the King of the Kingdom knows your circumstances. Our relationship with God has nothing to do with what happens to us as it relates to trials, tests, challenges, and assumed disappointments. The Lord doesn't spare us from the hardships of life just because we are citizens of the Kingdom. On the contrary, He allows trials for the purpose of testing, strengthening, and purifying our faith. Learning to persevere through hardship molds and matures our character.

If you find this idea hard to accept, consider the experience of Daniel. How would you feel if you were in Daniel's place and had just been told that because of your faithful obedience to God you were going to be thrown into a den full of hungry lions? Maybe Daniel prayed for deliverance and expected an angel to come. No angel showed up. Perhaps Daniel then thought that he would be translated supernaturally to safety, vanishing before the very eyes of King Darius and his court. No vanishing took place.

As they led Daniel in chains toward the lion's den, he may have thought that God would catch him halfway down the hall, loosen his chains, and set him free. It didn't happen. By the time he heard the growling of the lions, Daniel may have begun to wonder where God was. When he was thrown into the den and surrounded by hungry lions, he found out where God was—right there in the den with him! God had sent an angel ahead of Daniel to shut the lions' mouths, so that no harm would come to his servant. He saved Daniel, but not until Daniel had faced the trial of the lions' den without knowing the outcome beforehand. Where was God? Daniel had to shift his trust from the works of God to God Himself. (For the full story, see Daniel chapter 6.)

Daniel's quality of Kingdom faith is very rare today in the religious community as many of our contemporary doctrines and belief systems promote a shallow version of faith that focuses more on "avoidance faith" than enduring and overcoming faith. It is a faith built on avoiding troubles, trials, and tests rather than facing, enduring, and overcoming these temporary opportunities to prove the eternal power of our Kingdom. We need the faith of Daniel to be restored to our world today.

The same was true for Shadrach, Meshach, and Abednego, who had to endure a fiery furnace before they found their deliverance and discovered that God was with them in the fire (see Daniel chapter 3). This story of these three young Hebrew professionals should serve as a source of great encouragement and an outstanding example of true Kingdom faith. Let's recount some of the details of their encounter with the government of another kingdom and see the superiority of the currency of their faith as it activated the economy of God in their favor:

> *Then the king ordered Ashpenaz, chief of his court*
> *officials, to bring in some of the Israelites from the*
> *royal family and the nobility—young men without any*
> *physical defect, handsome, showing aptitude for every*
> *kind of learning, well informed, quick to understand,*
> *and qualified to serve in the king's palace. He was*

to teach them the language and literature of the
Babylonians. The king assigned them a daily amount
of food and wine from the king's table. They were to
be trained for three years, and after that they were to
enter the king's service.

Among these were some from Judah: Daniel,
Hananiah, Mishael and Azariah. The chief official gave
them new names: to Daniel, the name Belteshazzar;
to Hananiah, Shadrach; to Mishael, Meshach; and to
Azariah, Abednego (Daniel 1:3-7).

Moreover, at Daniel's request the king appointed
Shadrach, Meshach and Abednego administrators
over the province of Babylon, while Daniel himself
remained at the royal court (Daniel 2:49).

…So these men were brought before the king, and
Nebuchadnezzar said to them, "Is it true, Shadrach,
Meshach and Abednego, that you do not serve my
gods or worship the image of gold I have set up? Now
when you hear the sound of the horn, flute, zither,
lyre, harp, pipes and all kinds of music, if you are ready
to fall down and worship the image I made, very
good. But if you do not worship it, you will be thrown
immediately into a blazing furnace. Then what god
will be able to rescue you from my hand?"

Shadrach, Meshach and Abednego replied to the
king, "O Nebuchadnezzar, we do not need to defend

*ourselves before you in this matter. If we are thrown
into the blazing furnace, the God we serve is able
to save us from it, and He will rescue us from your
hand, O king. **But even if He does not,** we want you
to know, O king, that we will not serve your gods or
worship the image of gold you have set up"*
(Daniel 3:13-18).

The amazing thing about the faith of these young Kingdom citizens was their expression of belief that even if God did not rescue them, the integrity of the Kingdom of God remained intact. This is true Kingdom faith and must be restored in our daily lives in the Kingdom. We need faith that is stable even when our expectation of God's strategy is miscalculated, faith that is willing to be burned in the fire, proving its eternal nature. As the Kingdom ambassador, the apostle Peter said,

*In this you greatly rejoice, though now for a little while
you may have had to suffer grief in all kinds of trials.
These have come so that your faith—of greater worth
than gold, which perishes even though refined by
fire—may be proved genuine and may result in praise,
glory and honor when Jesus Christ is revealed*
(1 Peter 1:6-7).

The more your faith is tested, the more your Kingdom confidence grows. This is also true in the experience of the hurricanes in the Caribbean where I live. Every time we survive a major hurricane, the less fear and trauma we have in facing the next one until we come to see them as a normal part of life in our region and actually appreciate the benefits of such natural phenomenon. Hurricanes remove structures not built to government code, destroy rotten trees, cleanse pollutants in the air, and inspire new growth and new beginnings.

In the city of Philippi, Paul and Silas were beaten, thrown into prison, and locked into stocks for preaching the Gospel of Christ. Instead of whining and bemoaning their circumstances, they worshiped and sang hymns to God right there in the prison. God sent an earthquake that released all the prisoners. As a result, the jailer was converted to Christ along with his entire family (see Acts 16:16-34).

If our faith is in God, it doesn't matter what happens around us because God is stable. He never shifts or moves. He is the same yesterday, today, and forever (see Heb. 13:8). Jesus said, "*Eat My flesh. Don't 'eat' the things I give you; eat Me. Drink My blood. Don't 'drink' the blessings of life; drink Me. If you do, you will have life*" (see John 6:53-57). When our faith is in Him, we can endure anything because we trust in His power, not our own, and because He will not allow us to be tested beyond our ability to endure: "*No temptation has seized you except what is common to man. And God is faithful; He will not let you be tempted beyond what you can bear. But when you are tempted, He will also provide a way out so that you can stand up under it*" (1 Cor. 10:13).

How strong are you? *You are as strong as whatever your faith survives.* Kingdom faith will always be tested; that's how it grows strong. Just as muscles develop strength the more they are used, so too our faith gets stronger the more we exercise it. The greatest tests of faith—and therefore the greatest potential for growth—come during times of hardship. So if you trust in the Lord, get ready for the tests. Examination day is coming. *If you were to lose a job or a house, or if your child were sick and continued prayer produced no observable results, would you still believe in God's omniscient goodness? Would you still be confident in the overshadowing government of Heaven in the affairs of your life? That is Kingdom faith!*

Will You Pass the Test?

In the Kingdom of God, many citizens only follow the King for the good times and the good things. In fact the majority of the people I have encountered in the Christian religious community seem to have a relationship with God based on how they can benefit personally, rather than living as a citizen in a country with responsibilities, obligations, and commitments to obey the laws, maintain community, and function according to the principles of Kingdom society. Many religious believers treat God as a genie in a bottle whom they manipulate to meet their private wishes. This was the attitude of the people in the village of Capernaum when Jesus visited them after providing them with free bread and fish. Let us revisit that encounter:

> *Jesus answered, "I tell you the truth, you are looking*
> *for me, not because you saw miraculous signs but*
> *because you ate the loaves and had your fill. Do not*
> *work for food that spoils, but for food that endures*
> *to eternal life, which the Son of Man will give you. On*
> *Him God the Father has placed His seal of approval."*
> *Then they asked Him, "What must we do to do the*
> *works God requires?" Jesus answered, "The work of*
> *God is this: to believe in the one He has sent"*
> *(John 6:26-29).*

His assessment of their motive for following Him was for what they could get from Him. They had no concept of Kingdom citizenship and their obligation to serve the Kingdom despite of any condition. The King's statement, "do not work for bread that spoils" implies that belief in God should not be motivated by the positive benefits we can derive from that relationship, but by the character and nature of the benevolent King who loves His citizens. Consider these words as Jesus continues His discourse:

> I tell you the truth, he who believes has everlasting life.
> I am the bread of life. Your forefathers ate the manna
> in the desert, yet they died. But here is the bread that
> comes down from heaven, which a man may eat and
> not die. I am the living bread that came down from
> heaven. If anyone eats of this bread, he will live forever.
> This bread is My flesh, which I will give for the life of the
> world (John 6:47-51).

He was testing the quality and object of their faith and correcting their misplaced focus.

Many of the people in Capernaum with Jesus that day failed the faith test. After all, the call to Kingdom faith is a call to rise to challenges, overcome obstacles, and triumph over hardships, and many people simply are unwilling to pay the price. This certainly was true of many in Capernaum who were put off by Jesus' call to eat His flesh and drink His blood.

> On hearing it, many of His disciples said, "This is a hard
> teaching. Who can accept it?"
>
> From this time many of His disciples turned back and
> no longer followed Him. "You do not want to leave too,
> do you?" Jesus asked the Twelve.
>
> Simon Peter answered Him, "Lord, to whom shall we
> go? You have the words of eternal life. We believe and

know that You are the Holy One of God"
(John 6:60,66-69).

Why did the people consider Jesus' words a "hard teaching?" Because they realized He was calling them to follow Him with no guarantees of fish and bread; calling them to be satisfied with Him and Him alone; calling them to follow Him without knowing outcomes in advance, content to leave the future in His hands.

Once again Shadrach, Meshach, and Abednego demonstrated this kind of faith when they stood before King Nebuchadnezzar, threatened with death in a fiery furnace for refusing to obey the king's command to worship a great idol he had built. The arrogant king demanded to know what god could rescue them from his hand:

> *Shadrach, Meshach, and Abednego replied to the*
> *king, "O Nebuchadnezzar, we do not need to defend*
> *ourselves before you in this matter. If we are thrown*
> *into the blazing furnace, the God we serve is able to*
> *save us from it, and He will rescue us from your hand,*
> *O king. But even if He does not, we want you to know,*
> *O king, that we will not serve your gods or worship the*
> *image of gold you have set up (Daniel 3:16-18).*

That's Kingdom faith: faith that trusts God whether He blesses or not, whether He delivers or not, whether He heals or not. Kingdom faith trusts Christ no matter what because it knows that He has the "words of eternal life," and has discovered the same truth expressed by King David who wrote, *"Because Your love is better than life, my lips will glorify You"* (Ps. 63:3).

In the Kingdom of God when you don't know what to do, trust God! In another psalm, David declared, *"The Lord is my rock, my fortress, and my deliverer; my God is my rock, in whom I take refuge. He is my shield and the horn of my salvation, my stronghold"* (Ps. 18:2). If you are anchored on the rock, the storm doesn't matter. If your trust is in the living God, you are going to win no matter what happens around you. Many of Jesus' disciples turned back from following Him. *Many today have done the same.* Why? They were "fish sandwich" disciples. They turned back because Jesus took away their fish and bread and gave them His flesh and blood instead. They didn't want Him. He took away the gifts and gave them the Giver. They didn't want Him. He took away salvation and gave them the Savior. They didn't want Him. He took away the blessings and gave them the Blesser. They didn't want Him. *In a kingdom, the king is more important than the kingdom, for it is from him that the kingdom derives its legitimacy. The kingdom does not make the king a king, but the king makes the kingdom a kingdom.*

We are not here on earth just to get fish and bread. We are here to change the world by feeding others the living bread. Where is your faith? Is it in the works of God or in the God who works? Are you a "fish and bread" Christian or a "flesh and blood" believer? Your answer will determine whether your faith fails the test or stands firm through every storm.

Here in the Bahamas where we enjoy the beauty and quality of life of this tropical paradise, the government cannot guarantee immunity from hurricanes, storms, or other natural disasters, but it does guarantee protection, provision, resources, and restoration where necessary. The country and colony of the Kingdom of Heaven on earth is no different. The King, Jesus the Christ, does not guarantee immunity against test and trials; as a matter of fact, He guarantees they will come. Jesus said,

> *Therefore everyone who hears these words of Mine*
> *and puts them into practice is like a wise man who*

built his house on the rock. The rain came down, the streams rose, and the winds blew and beat against that house; yet it did not fall, because it had its foundation on the rock. But everyone who hears these words of Mine and does not put them into practice is like a foolish man who built his house on sand. The rain came down, the streams rose, and the winds blew and beat against that house, and it fell with a great crash (Matthew 7:24-27).

Kingdom faith is not afraid of storms, tests, and trials because citizens have built according to the construction code of the heavenly government and have ensured that their foundation is the unmovable rock of the integrity of the King's Word, character, and promises. Kingdom faith is anchored on the rock of Jesus Christ. Kingdom faith is faith that faces the storm and still stands firm after the storm has passed. Where is your faith?

Kingdom Principles

Your faith is only as strong as the tests it survives.

The question of Kingdom faith: "Can you follow the light even in the dark?"

In the Kingdom of God, the issue is not how much faith you have, but where your faith is placed.

The principle of Kingdom faith is to trust the Source and not the resource.

In the Kingdom of God, when you don't know what to do, trust God!

REDISCOVERING FAITH

Endnote

1. Reinhold Niebuhr, "Serenity Prayer" (1943); see http://www
   .yalealumnimagazine.com/issues/2008_07/serenity.html.

CHAPTER TWO

FAITH: THE CULTURE OF THE KINGDOM

"Faith consists in believing when it is beyond the power of reason to believe."

The message of the Bible is not about a religion, a fraternity, a burial society, or a ritualistic social club. An honest and objective look at the biblical text will reveal that this time-tested book is about a King and a Kingdom. Words like *king, lord, dominion, sovereignty, royalty, reign, glory, worship, adore, honor, throne, diadem, rule, obey,* and *bow down* are not words one would find in the culture or vocabulary of a democracy or a republic. These concepts are not found in the experience of our contemporary society, and perhaps this why the Bible is so difficult for many in our modern culture to understand or appreciate.

I was born in 1954 under a kingdom which had ruled our islands for over 200 years. The islands of the Bahamas were considered a colony of the king and kingdom of Great Britain which ruled many territories in the Caribbean region such as Jamaica, Barbados, Trinidad and Tobago, the British Virgin Islands, Granada, British Guyana, and many others.

What is a kingdom? Ideally a kingdom is the sovereign government and governing influence of a king over his territory impacting it with his purpose, his will, his nature, his laws, values, morals, and his culture, producing a citizenry reflecting his lifestyle. Therefore a kingdom is a nation or a country ruled by a king whose culture and society reflects the king's personal nature.

When a kingdom expands its kingdom influence to a distant territory, that process is called colonization. The goal of colonization is the extension of the kingdom's laws, values, and culture to the distant territory manifesting the glory of that king in that land. All kingdoms consist of the following: a king, a lord, domain or territory, a common language, a royal constitution, royal law, norms and values, morals, a royal code of ethics, royal protocol, an economy, a common welfare, and a unique culture that reflects the nature of the king.

This is the essence of the message and mandate of the Bible; a Kingdom and its text, purpose, interpretation, and application cannot be fully understood outside this context. Even a casual review of the message and priority of Jesus Christ reveals this truth:

> From that time on Jesus began to preach, "Repent, for the kingdom of heaven is near" (Matthew 4:17).

> Jesus went throughout Galilee, teaching in their synagogues, preaching the good news of the kingdom, and healing every disease and sickness among the people (Matthew 4:23).

> Blessed are the poor in spirit, for theirs is the kingdom of heaven (Matthew 5:3).

This, then, is how you should pray: "Our Father in heaven, hallowed be Your name, Your kingdom come, Your will be done on earth as it is in heaven" (Matthew 6:9-10).

But seek first His kingdom and His righteousness, and all these things will be given to you as well (Matthew 6:33).

Jesus went through all the towns and villages, teaching in their synagogues, preaching the good news of the kingdom and healing every disease and sickness (Matthew 9:35).

As you go, preach this message: "The kingdom of heaven is near." Heal the sick, raise the dead, cleanse those who have leprosy, drive out demons. Freely you have received, freely give (Matthew 10:7-8).

But if I drive out demons by the Spirit of God, then the kingdom of God has come upon you (Matthew 12:28).

He replied, "The knowledge of the secrets of the kingdom of heaven has been given to you, but not to them" (Matthew 13:11).

Listen then to what the parable of the sower means: When anyone hears the message about the kingdom and does not understand it, the evil one comes

and snatches away what was sown in his heart…
(Matthew 13:18-19).

He told them still another parable: "The kingdom of heaven is like yeast that a woman took and mixed into a large amount of flour until it worked all through the dough" (Matthew 13:33).

I will give you the keys of the kingdom of heaven; whatever you bind on earth will be bound in heaven, and whatever you loose on earth will be loosed in heaven (Matthew 16:19).

And this gospel of the kingdom will be preached in the whole world as a testimony to all nations, and then the end will come (Matthew 24:14).

The above are only a few examples of the message of Jesus and detail the priority of the Kingdom concept to His mission on earth. Jesus came to earth to restore the Kingdom colony of Heaven on earth which was God's original purpose and mandate for human-kind. The fall of humankind resulted in the loss of the Kingdom government of Heaven on earth. It was this mandate that motivated God the Creator to send His Son the King back to the colony to restore the influence, laws, values, lifestyle, and culture of Heaven back to earth. The Kingdom and culture of Heaven can only be appropriated by the heavenly citizens through the currency of faith. According to the King, the promises and privileges of life in the Kingdom must be activated by the quality of faith. One of the principle keys of the Kingdom is faith.

> *...According to your faith will it be done to you*
> (Matthew 9:29).

Faith is one of the most abused, misused, and misunderstood concepts in human life. Throughout history faith has been perceived in many different ways, both inside and outside religion. In the name of faith, people have raped, pillaged, plundered, oppressed, and murdered on a massive scale. Over the past 100 years more people have been killed for their faith *and in the name of faith* than in every preceding century of history combined. And in many cases, those doing the killing did so with the belief that they were serving God.

Even within the Christian church, faith has been abused and mis-appropriated for selfish gain so often that it has been attacked and held in contempt by those who don't understand it. For the same reason faith has become almost eradicated from the experience of many believers. True faith is a gift from God, and the Bible contains many warnings against using God's gifts for personal gain.

The phrase "Kingdom faith," as used in this book, was chosen deliberately to distinguish it from "faith" in its more general meaning. "Kingdom faith" is the same as "true faith," the faith that characterizes life not in "religion," but in the Kingdom of God. It is the shared culture of all true citizens of the Kingdom.

Once again let me stress, *the Kingdom of God is not a religion; Christianity is a religion.* The Kingdom of God is a *country.* When Jesus began His public teaching ministry, He came not as a preacher hawking a new religion but as an ambassador speaking on behalf of His Father's government. He did not say, "Behold I announce to you a new religion." No, the first recorded words of Jesus were these: "*Repent, for the kingdom of heaven is near*" (Matt. 4:17b).

Throughout the Bible in both the Old and New Testaments, the message of the Kingdom of God is a message about a country. Deep in our hearts, every human being is searching for a better country than the one we live in on earth. All human governments are flawed. Even the best and most beneficent of them fail to satisfy our deepest longings. Our search for a better country is perfectly natural. After all, we didn't lose a religion when Adam and Eve fell in the Garden of Eden—we lost a country. We lost a dominion. We lost a kingdom. We lost a culture. Kingdom faith is the key to regaining what we lost. So when I use the term "Kingdom faith," I am talking about faith in the context of a country.

Kingdom Faith Culture

Every country has a culture, and the Kingdom of God is no exception. *Culture* refers to the particular beliefs, moral values, social customs, and lifestyles that distinguish a nation or people group as unique. Kingdom faith is the distinctive characteristic of Kingdom citizens, so we can say that faith is the culture of the Kingdom of God. From the very beginning God intended the citizens of His Kingdom to have a cultural faith. But what does this mean?

First of all, it means that *faith is the currency of the Kingdom of God.* Currency refers to whatever is used as legal tender in a country. No country can function without currency. In order to live, trade, buy, and sell in a country, it is necessary to have the currency of that country. What happens if you don't have the right currency? You can't buy anything. You cannot purchase food, drink, shelter, goods, or services. No matter how much money you may have in your pocket, if it is the wrong currency for where you are, you are as good as broke. Without the proper currency, you are unable to function at anything more than a bare subsistence level, and sometimes not even that.

What do we call people who don't have any currency? We call them poor. In earthly cultures, poor people are the people who have no money. In the Kingdom of God, however, poverty is measured not in terms of lack of money, but in lack of faith. People without faith are poor in God's Kingdom regardless of how much money is in their bank account. When a rich young man asked Jesus what he had to do to find eternal life, Jesus replied, *"If you want to be perfect, go, sell all your possessions and give to the poor, and you will have treasure in heaven. Then come, follow Me"* (Matt. 19:21).

Essentially Jesus was saying to the man, "Don't trust in your riches; trust in Me. Then you will find true wealth." Earthly riches will not last. Kingdom faith is the real treasure. *Why is faith more important than earthly wealth? Wealth is always temporary and can be stolen, lost, or can depreciate in value as it has in the 2008-2009 global economic crisis. But Kingdom faith is "access" to the unlimited store of the commonwealth of Heaven and can never be exhausted. If you lose your money, you are only depleted. If you lose your faith, you are completely defeated.*

The devil is not after your money. He's not after your house, your clothes, your children, or anything else you think he's after. He's after one thing—your faith. He knows that if he can steal your faith you will be spiritually bankrupt. Faith gives us hope, so if faith is lost, hope flees away like mist in the wind. Loss of faith leads to loss of hope, which leads to despair. Life becomes pointless and without value. In fact, we could say that despair characterizes the lives of most of the people in the world. The poorest person on earth is the person without faith.

Currency is necessary for quality of life in any country. The amount of currency you have determines how much you can do in a society. Faith is the currency of the Kingdom of God. Without it you can get nothing and do nothing. Without faith, the life and riches of God's Kingdom are closed to you.

This brings us to the second point about Kingdom faith culture: *everything in the Kingdom is received by faith.* How many things? *Everything.* Is that hard to understand? Then let's turn it around: *nothing* in the Kingdom is received *without* faith. This is a critically important concept. Without currency you can do nothing. In fact, one of the fundamental principles of commerce and finance is that you have to *have* money in order to get money or make money. That is why a bank will not give you a loan unless you can come up with 10 or 20 percent of the amount on your own as a down payment. Remember Jesus' question, *"When the Son of Man comes, will He find faith on the earth?"* (Luke 18:8b). When Jesus returns, will the whole earth be bankrupt of the most important currency of all? Everything in the Kingdom is received by faith, and nothing in the Kingdom is received without it.

If faith is the currency of the Kingdom, then *faith is necessary for living in the Kingdom.* As I said before, if we lose faith, we are spiritually bankrupt, which leaves us unequipped and unsuited for Kingdom life. Satan attacks just to steal our faith. He did it with Job, so why wouldn't he do it with you and me? Why would satan cause your house to burn down? So you will stop trusting God. Why would he put sickness in your body and attack you with disease? So you will stop believing that God can heal. Why would he bring financial reversal into your life? So you will stop believing God can provide for your needs. Satan is after our faith because he knows that we live by it in our country. We spend faith on things in the Kingdom of God. It's the way we live.

Faith is necessary in the Kingdom of God because *without faith the Kingdom principles cannot be activated.* Every country has a constitution. In the Kingdom of God, the constitution is the Bible. A constitution contains the precepts by which the country functions. In order for a country's citizens to function effectively and enjoy the full benefits of their citizenship, it is important that they understand their nation's laws and how they work. In the Kingdom of God, faith activates the laws. Without faith, nothing we read in the constitution can come to pass. Apart from faith, the laws, promises, and revelations of the Word of God are only words on a page. Faith brings them to life as the Spirit of faith quickens them in our hearts. This is why even some people who are not believers can read the Bible, study it, and even quote it as well or better than you or I, yet it has no positive effect on their lives because faith activates the law. Faith is the currency that activates all the promises and principles of the Kingdom. We cannot truly live a Kingdom life unless we understand and use faith properly.

To sum up then, *faith is the lifestyle of the Kingdom.* In other words, faith is the style that we live by, the style we wear like a garment. It is the way we manifest Kingdom culture. Faith keeps us alive.

Faith Defined

The word *faith* is used to describe many concepts in life. For example, "the faith" usually refers to a formal set of beliefs or an established religion such "the Christian faith." To "keep the faith" means to hold firmly to your belief system or religious commitment. The term "faith movement" refers to an adherence to a belief system that magnifies the power of belief to the status of a doctrine. All of these are legitimate expressions that serve to define individual and corporate experiences of millions over time.

The concept of faith has been of great interest throughout history but especially in the past 40 years, and it has even been the subject of doctrinal exploration, producing major religious movements and organizations. The revival of the focus on faith which gave rise to what in the Western world is known as "the faith movement" has had a very positive impact on the lives of millions of believers around the world. This rediscovery of faith as a major component in the Western religious experience has brought many back to the importance of faith in humankind's relationship with God. I, too, have benefited greatly from this focus.

However, there has also been a not-so-positive impact from this emphasis. For many, faith has become an isolated doctrine, creating an exclusive believers' club that leaves those who don't have the "right kind of faith" feeling spiritually inadequate. This has had a devastating effect on millions, causing many to lead lives of guilt, frustration, depression, and low self-esteem—or turn "from the faith" completely. The paradox of it all is that faith was intended to eradicate these very destructive elements. Faith, which is supposed to breed hope, produces instead a sense of deficiency.

Perhaps the real problem is that faith was never intended to be a doctrine or an isolated message but rather a natural experience integrated within the bigger picture of God's plan for humankind. Jesus Christ Himself never taught faith as an isolated component but always in the context of His principal message: the Kingdom. His position seemed to be that faith is a normal part of life in the Kingdom. In essence the concept of faith must not be separated from the context of the Kingdom and can only have its full effect in its vital role of appropriating the promises of the government of Heaven on earth.

But what exactly is faith? How do we define it in a way that is truly meaningful? The writer of the New Testament Book of Hebrews defined it this way: "*Now faith is being sure of what we hope for and certain of what we do not see*" (Heb. 11:1). In Hebrew the most common word for faith is `aman, while the Greek word for faith used most often in the New Testament is *pistis*.[1] Essentially, *pistis* means belief, but more than just casual mental assent or acceptance. *Pistis* refers to conviction, a deeply-held belief. It also means "persuaded." Someone who has *pistis* faith is persuaded at a deep level of conviction that something is true.

Another way to describe *pistis* is to say that it is a faith of confident expectation. This is what Hebrews 11:1 means. Confident expectation is "being sure of what we hope for and certain of what we do not see." We cannot have true faith and not expect something to happen. With *pistis* faith we confidently expect and patiently wait for God to act for our good and His glory, even when we can see no visible evidence of anything happening.

True faith also means a "sure hope." But isn't that a contradiction in terms? Not from a biblical perspective. We tend to think of hope as something we desire but have no certainty that we will receive: "I hope I get that new job." Biblical hope is different. Biblical hope is sure and certain because it is anchored on the integrity and promises of God. We may not see it yet, but we know it is coming because God said so. The apostle Paul said of hope, *"For in this hope we were saved. But hope that is seen is no hope at all. Who hopes for what he already has? But if we hope for what we do not yet have, we wait for it patiently"* (Rom. 8:24-25). And once again, the writer of Hebrews, *"We have this hope as an anchor for the soul, firm and secure. It enters the inner sanctuary behind the curtain where Jesus, who went before us, has entered on our behalf"* (Heb. 6:19-20a). Hope is a vital part of Kingdom faith, and because it is anchored on God who cannot lie and who never changes, it is as sure for us as if we already held it in our hands.

Because it is based on this kind of hope, *pistis* faith also means "resolve." To resolve is to come to a definite decision or conclusion about something. Resolve says, "I know God will keep His word. I don't know how, when, or where He will do it, but one thing I do know, He *will* do it!"

The tragedy for much of the modern Church is that the faith of many professed believers does not rise to this level. What about yours? Are you trusting in wealth, circumstances, and things you can see, or is your faith anchored in the Person of Jesus Christ, who cannot lie and who is *"the same yesterday and today and forever"* (Heb. 13:8)?

Let's see how this works. If you expect it to rain, what do you do? You carry an umbrella. The sky may be clear and the sun shining, but if the weather forecast calls for showers, and you believe it, you will leave the house prepared for rain. People may see you walking with your umbrella on a bright and sunny day and think you are crazy, but you may know something they don't, and you are ready for it. When you have faith, you prepare in advance for the answer because you know it's coming. Some people say they trust God to care for them but do nothing to prepare themselves for the future or for the storms that are sure to come. That's not faith; it's presumption. It's foolishness.

Faith is sure hope that drives you to action. That's why the Bible says that faith without works is dead (see James 2:26). Actions or good works are no substitute for faith. True faith—Kingdom faith—*results* in actions and good works. Kingdom faith *produces* good works, not the other way around. The purpose for this book is not to focus primarily on the definition of faith, which can be obtained through a myriad of books and courses available from many sources. My principal purpose in this work is to restore faith to the context of the bigger picture of the Kingdom of Heaven and the extension of that Kingdom to earth—to purge faith from its extreme isolation and reset it in the culture and nature of Kingdom living. *Faith is to the Kingdom like oxygen is to humankind, like money is to the economy, like water is to fish. It's necessary, but not extraordinary. Without faith you cannot do business with the government of the Kingdom of Heaven. The principle of Kingdom faith is simple: "You cannot appropriate what you don't believe; you cannot inspect what you do not expect." Just as you cannot live within the economy of your country without money, so you cannot live in the Kingdom of God without the currency of faith.*

Kingdom Faith in Action

Kingdom faith gives us access to all the rights, privileges, and benefits of the Kingdom of God—everything promised in the constitution, the Bible. This is why it is so important that we understand that Kingdom faith is—and must be—a lifestyle. Citizens with the right currency can obtain anything the Kingdom has to offer. All they have to do is ask. Let's look at an example from the New Testament.

> *As Jesus went on from there, two blind men followed Him, calling out, "Have mercy on us, Son of David!"*
>
> *When He had gone indoors, the blind men came to Him, and He asked them, "Do you believe that I am able to do this?"*
>
> *"Yes, Lord," they replied.*
>
> *Then He touched their eyes and said, "According to your faith will it be done to you"; and their sight was restored* (Matthew 9:27-30a).

There is nothing mysterious about Kingdom faith. It is straightforward, practical, and has nothing to do with religion or religious ritual. When these two blind men came to Jesus seeking their sight, He did not ask them any religious questions. He didn't ask them how many prayers they had prayed or how much money they had given to the Temple treasury. He asked one simple, non-religious question: "Do you believe that I am able to do this?" That was it. Essentially Jesus asked them, "Can you pay the price to get your eyesight back?" Remember that faith is the currency of the Kingdom. These two blind men were seeking a Kingdom benefit—wholeness of body—but they needed the right currency. And that currency was faith. To put it another way, Jesus said to them, "Do you want your eyesight back? Show Me your money." And they said, "Here it is, Lord: we believe." And Jesus said, "OK, that's enough." And He restored their sight. They transacted Kingdom business with Kingdom currency and got what they were after.

Kingdom faith is really nothing more than citizens of the Kingdom *believing their government's legal promises in the constitution of the Word* and *claiming their rights under the law.* Notice how the two blind men addressed Jesus. First they called Him the "Son of David," acknowledging that Jesus was a King because He was descended from David's kingly line. "Son of David" was also a phrase that in Jesus' day was understood to refer to the Messiah, Israel's promised King and Deliverer. The blind men also called Jesus "Lord," which means "owner." In using that title they were acknowledging that Jesus was indeed King and the rightful owner of all things, including them-selves. By calling Jesus "Lord," they were saying, in effect, "You own us, and we're blind, which means that you own blindness." This put pressure on Jesus, because a king's reputation rests in part on the welfare and quality of the life of his people. These two men came as Kingdom citizens to claim their Kingdom right of wellness, paid with the currency of faith, and went away whole.

Some people come to God to get things, but they don't want God to own them. "Bless me, Lord, but don't get involved in my life. Don't touch my relationships. Don't get involved in my business." But God says, "Wait a minute. Who do you think I am?" That is a critical question. Who is God to you? To "religious" faith, God is a celestial Santa Claus to whom they go to get things. To Kingdom faith, however, God is Lord and King, sovereign Creator and Owner of all things.

Jesus said, *"Therefore I tell you, whatever you ask for [desire] in prayer, believe that you have received it, and it will be yours"* (Mark 11:24). Many people misunderstand and abuse this verse thinking that it means they can selfishly demand anything they want from God. They are wrong. Scripture also states that we must ask in Jesus' name (see John 14:13), which means in accordance with His character, and that we must ask in accordance with God's will (see 1 John 5:14). Whereas casual interest displays a "take-it-or-leave-it" attitude, desire has to do with deep passion. Desire is the inner drive that says, "I'm not going to let it go until I get it." Jesus asked the two blind men, "Do you believe that I am able to do this?" Unspoken but implied was another question: "How badly do you want it?" The degree to which we receive in the Kingdom is determined by the degree to which we believe. The more faith we exercise (the more currency we trade), the fuller will be our experience of Kingdom life. If we lose faith, we can get nothing from the Kingdom of God. That is why satan is after our faith.

The Enemies of Faith

In his relentless campaign to destroy our faith, satan employs two powerful weapons, two devastating enemies of faith: fear and doubt. Fear and doubt are related. Whenever one shows up, the other is never far behind. One of satan's top faith-stealing strategies is to try to sow fear into our lives. He will do all sorts of drastic things and bring all manner of adversity across our paths in order to make us afraid because he knows that where there is fear there is no faith.

Fear produces *torment*, and torment stirs up hopelessness, a feeling that there is no way out of the current torment. Another word for torment is *worry*. Prolonged, unrelieved worry causes all sorts of health problems. In fact, worry is the number one factor at the base of nearly every disease. So fear can actually make us physically sick. The last thing we want in life is to give in to fear. Living in fear destroys our potential and debilitates our faith.

Living in faith, on the other hand, will empower us to reach our fullest potential and even do the impossible. One day, as an object lesson to His disciples, Jesus cursed a fig tree that bore no fruit. Immediately the tree withered. In amazement, the disciples asked how this had happened:

> Jesus replied, "I tell you the truth, if you have faith and do not doubt, not only can you do what was done to the fig tree, but also you can say to this mountain, 'Go, throw yourself into the sea,' and it will be done. If you believe, you will receive whatever you ask for in prayer" (Matthew 21:21-22).

As long as we try to live under Kingdom culture in this world, we will always have to battle between faith and fear. Our challenge is to make sure that faith wins. Fear will keep us away from the mountain; faith will move the mountain. I don't think Jesus was talking about physical mountains necessarily, although that too might be a possibility. What He was talking about is anything that *looks* like a mountain to us, anything that seems to be impassable, that seems to block our progress. Kingdom faith will drive all obstacles away. They may not all disappear at once, but ultimately faith will win out. Faith is the victory that overcomes the world.

We make prayer out to be so hard, but in Kingdom culture it should be the most natural thing in the world. Consider the simplicity of Jesus' statement: *"If you believe, you will receive whatever you ask for in prayer."* What could be simpler? It's straightforward and precise. The only requirement for effectiveness in prayer is faith. If you believe, if you exercise Kingdom faith, then not even satan and all the powers of hell can stop you. Fear cannot stand in the presence of faith. By faith we know that God is love and that He loves us. Faith teaches us to love God, and as this love relationship grows, fear flees because love drives out fear: *"There is no fear in love. But perfect love drives out fear, because fear has to do with punishment. The one who fears is not made perfect in love"* (1 John 4:18).

Kingdom faith must overcome doubt and tests. Everyone on earth goes through tests. Trials and troubles are the common lot of humankind. None of us are immune; none of us are exempt. While we may have no control over when, where, and how the tests come, we do have control over how we respond to them. Tests will either make or break our faith. More to the point, tests will prove or reveal what kind of faith we have. Kingdom faith that is anchored on the rock of Christ will stand; any other kind of faith will not. Whenever we face a crisis of some kind, we have to make a choice between faith and fear. Jesus understands this, which is why He so often said, "Don't be afraid."

One day a synagogue leader named Jairus asked Jesus to come to his house and heal his daughter who was very sick. While they were on the way, messengers arrived to inform them that the girl had died. They then suggested that Jairus shouldn't "bother" Jesus anymore. Jesus thought differently: *"Ignoring what they said, Jesus told the synagogue ruler, 'Don't be afraid, just believe'"* (Mark 5:36). He then entered Jairus' house and brought his daughter back to life.

Guard your faith carefully. People will try to talk you out of your belief. Fear and doubt are the two great enemies, and they are always crouching just outside the door ready to pounce. Like everyone else, I have known fear and doubt, and I know how powerful they are. A doctor gives you the diagnosis: cancer. Your boss gives you the word that you are being laid off. Your house burns to the ground, and you lose everything. Something like this happens, and the ground drops from beneath your feet. Your whole world falls apart. Before you can even think about it, the fear wells up inside and threatens to overwhelm you. Jesus says, "I understand. I know you are afraid. Don't be. Trust in Me. Shift your fear into faith." In any crisis situation the choice is always there: fear or faith. Choose faith. It won't always be easy because fear will fight you tooth and nail, but don't give up. Fight back. Fight the fight of faith.

The Fight of Faith

The fight between faith and fear is the only fight we really have in life. We don't even fight the devil; he just tries to make us think we are. The apostle Paul urged Timothy, his young protégé, to *"Fight the good fight of the faith"* (1 Tim. 6:12a). Paul also practiced what he preached. Toward the end of his life, Paul testified to Timothy, *"I have fought the good fight, I have finished the race, I have kept the faith"* (2 Tim. 4:7). Concerning the nature of this fight, Paul wrote, *"For our struggle is not against flesh and blood, but against the rulers, against the authorities, against the powers of this dark world and against the spiritual forces of evil in the heavenly realms"* (Eph. 6:12). Spiritual enemies call for spiritual weapons:

> *For though we live in the world, we do not wage war*
> *as the world does. The weapons we fight with are not*
> *the weapons of the world. On the contrary, they have*

divine power to demolish strongholds. We demolish arguments and every pretension that sets itself up against the knowledge of God, and we take captive every thought to make it obedient to Christ (2 Corinthians 10:3-5).

The "strongholds" Paul refers to are mental strongholds, entrenched ways of thinking that the devil uses to mislead us as to the nature of our fight as well as to the identities of our true enemies. The trials of life—sickness, job loss, financial reversal, rebellious children, and the like—are not our enemies. Our enemies are the evil spiritual powers of darkness that take advantage of trials to instill fear and doubt in our hearts with the purpose of causing us to lose hope. That is why we need divine power—Christ's power—to demolish those mental strongholds and replace them with new ways of thinking built on a foundation of faith.

Kingdom faith is so powerful that it even removes the fear of death. Both the Bible and subsequent history are filled with the testimonies of believers who faced death fearlessly, confidently, and even with joyful anticipation because in faith they knew that death was not an ending but a beginning. Physical death means nothing to a Kingdom citizen; it is merely the doorway to the other side, to life in its absolute fullness. As believers we don't lose when we die; we win. Sometimes we measure God by this side and forget that He's even greater on the other side. Paul knew this to be true, which is why he could write in perfect peace, "For to me, to live is Christ and to die is gain" (Phil. 1:21). Faith is the victory that leads to pure, complete, and total salvation. Don't let fear and doubt rule your life. They are faith robbers.

One reason why so many people have a problem with faith is because it appears counterintuitive; it seemingly goes against "rational" thought. The world tends to take external appearances and circumstances at face value. Looks are often deceiving, however. We can never know the truth about any situation until we can see it from God's perspective, and that requires faith. To the world faith makes no sense because it involves paradox. A paradox is an apparently contradictory statement that is nevertheless true. Kingdom life is built on paradoxes: the last shall be first and the first, last (see Matt. 19:30); the greatest in the Kingdom are servants of all (see Matt. 23:11); humility is the path to greatness (see Matt. 18:4); those who lose their life for Christ's sake shall save it (see Matt. 16:25). Faith too is a paradox. As Hebrews 11:1 tells us, faith is being *sure* of what we *hope* for and *certain* of what we *have not seen*. To put it another way, when in doubt, have faith; when you don't know what to do, believe; when nothing makes sense, trust.

As we saw in Chapter One, it matters where we place our faith. Jesus said, "*Have faith in God*" (Mark 11:22). Trust not in things or in people, but in God. He alone is unshakable. People will let you down. Systems will fail. Jobs will go away. Put your faith in God. His Kingdom will never fall. God will never fail you. He is steady. He is stable. God is forever.

Faith, Not Signs

As we have already seen, faith in God means trusting in His Person, not in His provision. It means believing in Him because of who He is, not because of what He does. Faith that always seeks signs is immature faith. Remember, Kingdom faith believes in what is *hoped for* and *not yet seen*.

One day when a man came to Jesus asking for a miracle, Jesus gave a surprising response:

*Once more He visited Cana in Galilee, where He had
turned the water into wine. And there was a certain
royal official whose son lay sick at Capernaum. When
this man heard that Jesus had arrived in Galilee from
Judea, he went to Him and begged Him to come and
heal his son, who was close to death.*

*"Unless you people see miraculous signs and wonders,"
Jesus told him, "you will never believe"* (John 4:46-48).

Doesn't that sound harsh? A fearful, heartsick man comes to Jesus
to ask for healing for his dying son, and Jesus says, "Unless you see a
miracle, you will not believe." Here's a man with a problem, and you
would think that Jesus would respond with compassion. Instead, he
offers a rebuke of faith that always seeks signs. Jesus certainly must
have been grieved many times over the lack of faith He encountered
in the people who flocked after Him. No doubt He was tired of them
coming to Him just to get things. But there was something else at
work here too. Jesus was testing both the faith and motivation of the
man who sought His help. The man passed the test.

*The royal official said, "Sir, come down before my
child dies."*

Jesus replied, "You may go. Your son will live."

*The man took Jesus at His word and departed. While
he was still on the way, his servants met him with the
news that his boy was living. When he inquired as to
the time his son got better, they said to him, "The fever
left him yesterday at the seventh hour."*

> *Then the father realized that this was the exact time at
> which Jesus has said to him, "Your son will live." So he
> and all his household believed* (John 4:49-53).

This grieving father's only concern was the life of his dying son. He wasn't after a flashy display or a spectacular miracle; he just wanted his son to be well again. *Now* Jesus responded with compassion. The test was over. He told the man to go home and assured him that his son would live. Notice that the man *took Jesus at His word and departed.* His original request was for Jesus to *come* and heal his son. Instead, Jesus said, *"Go. Your son will live."* This was enough for the man. His confident departure based on Jesus' assurance proved that his faith was not in miracles, but in the God of miracles. Verification of his son's healing at the exact moment Jesus announced it solidified the man's faith to the point that he and his entire household were converted. Like the two blind men, this grieving father transacted Kingdom business with Kingdom currency—faith—and received a Kingdom benefit.

Sometimes God wants us to fight for our faith because fighting for our faith strengthens it. Blessings don't always come when we want them; healings do not always occur on our timetable; hardships do not always go away as quickly as we would like. God uses these times to test our faith. He is asking, "Will you trust Me no matter what? Even if you don't get what you want when you want it or the way you want it, will you still believe?" He wants to see our faith at work. And He wants us to see that faith works.

It isn't miracles that keep us; it is the Word of God. The man with the sick son *believed Jesus' word*—and received his miracle. His faith was in Christ, not in what Christ could do. Remember, blessings are temporary. Miracles are temporary. Jesus raised Lazarus from the dead, but Lazarus died again later. Signs and wonders are temporary, but God is permanent.

The things that God wants to do in your life He cannot do without faith. You've got to believe in Him *alone*, apart from any signs. He will test your faith to prove it and make it strong. Sometimes He will take you right to the edge and say, "Jump." Will you jump with only His word to go on, trusting Him for the outcome? Or will you turn back and say, "First show me a sign, Lord!" He wants to know that you trust Him enough to jump. Even more, He wants *you* to know that you trust Him enough to jump. He may let you fall all the way to the ground before catching you, but He will catch you. Then He will say, "Good for you! I knew you could do it! You are truly a child of My Kingdom!"

Faith is the currency of the Kingdom. Spend it lavishly and everything will be open to you. Put your faith in God. Believe in Him and all things are possible.

Kingdom Principles

Faith is the currency of the Kingdom of God.

Everything in the Kingdom is received by faith.

Without faith the Kingdom principles cannot be activated.

The principle of Kingdom faith is simple: "You cannot appropriate what you don't believe; you cannot inspect what you do not expect."

Kingdom faith is really nothing more than citizens of the Kingdom believing their government's legal promises in the constitution of the Word and claiming their rights under the law.

*When in doubt, have faith; when you don't know what to do,
believe; when nothing makes sense, trust.*

Endnote

1. See http://www.studylight.org/lex/heb/view
   .cgi?number=0530; "`aman";
   http://www.studylight.org/lex/grk/view.cgi?number=4102;
   "*pistis.*"

CHAPTER THREE

KINGDOM FAITH
IS TESTED FAITH

"Faith isn't faith until it's all you're holding onto."

Kingdom faith is tested faith, and tested faith is mature faith. Remember, our faith is only as strong as the tests it survives. *You do not believe until you have to.* The strength of our faith determines how well we function in and enjoy the fullness of Kingdom life. Faith is the currency of the Kingdom of God, and Kingdom economy never suffers recession. It never experiences inflation. Kingdom economy is always stable, always safe, always secure. Whenever we invest our currency (faith) in Kingdom economy, we are always investing in a "bull market."

It is one thing to talk big about faith, but quite another to invest our faith—to "put our money where our mouth is"—during times of stress and testing. That is when our true level of maturity is revealed. Our maturity is measured by how we handle pressure, stress, and times of confusion and upheaval. Immature people collapse under stress. They give up under pressure. They quit when things get tough. How mature are you?

The key to effective living is the capacity and ability to manage the expected and *the unexpected.* For most people, dealing with the expected is not too difficult because it is easier to prepare for. But what about the unexpected? When something unexpected happens suddenly, how do you react? Your response to the unexpected is a telltale sign of what you are made of. Mature people prepare for the unexpected. They expect the unexpected and plan ahead for it. Immature people do not and usually suffer the consequences. In the words of an ancient proverb, *"A prudent man sees danger and takes refuge, but the simple keep going and suffer for it"* (Prov. 22:3).

Maturity and success are related. *Success is measured by your ability to maintain personal balance in times of turmoil.* I have a little saying that I have lived by for many years: "Since I'm not worrying, you can worry for me." There are enough people worrying about everything already, so why join them? Mature people maintain personal balance even during times of turmoil. Maintaining balance means believing what God said more than believing what we see. Remember, appearances can be deceiving. In any situation, we have to see through God's eyes before we know the truth. And to see we must use the eyes of faith. The greatest revelations in life, as well as the greatest opportunities for growth, always come during unexpected crises and times of testing. That is when God reveals Himself to us in fresh new ways. Because we need to handle new environments, He gives us new faith. But we have to exercise the faith we have.

Tests mold us and help us grow into mature, balanced individuals. *Maturity is measured by your capacity to respond effectively to tragedy and chaos.* How do you handle chaos? What do you do when suddenly everything collapses around you? Your actions in that moment will reveal how mature you are. We can always tell a person's maturity by how he or she handles pressure. To put it another way, we never truly know a person until we observe his or her behavior under stress. Pressure not only reveals maturity; it also reveals character. Can you rise to the occasion of the unexpected, the chaotic, even the tragic? Does your faith stand firm and grow under the tests of life? Or does your world have to remain neat, orderly, and unruffled in order for you to deal with life? Don't dread the tests; they will make you strong. All you have to do is stand firm in your faith, and you will come through with maturity and balance.

One encouragement we have for standing firm in our faith is the fact that we are citizens of a Kingdom which can never be thrown down or displaced. The Kingdom of God is an eternal kingdom that will still be standing in all its power and glory ages after the last human government has crumbled to dust. Let us take heart from the words of Scripture: *"Therefore, since we are receiving a kingdom that cannot be shaken, let us be thankful, and so worship God acceptably with reverence and awe, for our 'God is a consuming fire'"* (Heb. 12:28-29).

The country of Heaven and the government it represents cannot be shaken. Sometimes we forget what this Kingdom has already been through, and that it has been through worse things than we see it going through in our lifetime. Throughout the ages many human empires and governments have tried to destroy God's Kingdom. They have persecuted and killed God's people; banned and burned God's book, the Bible; outlawed the teaching of God's Word; and in many other ways tried to undermine, distort, and discredit the Kingdom of God. Yet one by one every one of those regimes have fallen and disappeared from the face of the earth while the Kingdom of God still stands firm and unshakeable. It's been through everything we could imagine and still emerges victorious—and always will. Every generation sees new powers or governments arise to challenge the sovereignty of God; we see them in our world today. This is to be expected because satan never gives up. But the Kingdom of God will outlast them all, so we have every reason to be confident.

Tested Faith Builds Endurance

Successful living in a world full of daily challenges calls for tough people who know how to endure. Kingdom faith builds endurance, not by avoiding or escaping tests and hardship, but by facing them down in the power of God's Spirit. The Word of God makes a clear link between faith and endurance through testing:

> We ought always to thank God for you, brothers, and rightly so, because your faith is growing more and more, and the love every one of you has for each other is increasing. Therefore, among God's churches we boast about your perseverance and faith in all the persecutions and trials you are enduring.
>
> All this is evidence that God's judgment is right, and as a result you will be counted worthy of the kingdom of God, for which you are suffering (2 Thessalonians 1:3-5).

The Christian believers in the city of Thessalonica were undergoing "persecutions and trials." They were "suffering," Paul said, for the Kingdom of God. And what was the result of their suffering? Were they surrendering, or fleeing, or giving in, or abandoning their faith? Hardly. On the contrary, they were "enduring." Their faith was "growing more and more," and their love for one another was increasing. All of this was taking place *in the midst* of trials and persecutions. These believers were developing a reputation for faith and perseverance. Wouldn't it be great for people to know you not for what you avoided, but for what you made it through? Whenever we endure trials with grace and confidence and emerge stronger on the other side, we encourage and inspire others to endure the tests they are facing. Even more, our endurance points them to Jesus, in whose strength we endure.

Kingdom faith equips us to endure trials and becomes stronger with every test we survive. That is the nature of Kingdom faith; it thrives in the crucible of crisis. We cannot escape the trials and tests of life, but we can prevail over them through the presence and power of the Lord. And we can experience inner peace at the same time. Jesus said, *"I have told you these things, so that in Me you may have peace. In this world you will have trouble. But take heart! I have overcome the world"* (John 16:33).

People generally aren't impressed by our faith during good times. Anyone can believe when things are going well. They are watching to see what we do when the going gets tough. Can you shine for Jesus wherever you are no matter what's happening in your life?

I will always remember the day years ago in Tulsa, Oklahoma, when I had lunch with Corrie ten Boom. Miss ten Boom and other members of her family, working out of her father's watch and clock shop in their native Holland, were instrumental in hiding Jews from the Nazis in World War II and helping them get out of the country. Eventually they were captured by the Germans and sent to concentration camps. Corrie's father and her sister Betsie both died in the camps. Before Betsie's death, however, she and Corrie spread the light of the love and grace of Christ among the women with whom they were imprisoned at the Ravensbruck concentration camp. Using a small Bible Corrie had successfully smuggled past the guards, they held nightly Bible readings and prayer meetings in their barracks.

The light of the truth of Heaven shone in a place that was hell on earth, and lives were changed eternally.

Released from Ravensbruck by a "clerical error" a month before all other women prisoners her age were sent to the gas chambers, Corrie spent the rest of her long life traveling the world, teaching and testifying to the grace and love of God. She used to say, "There is no pit so deep that God's love is not deeper still."[1] She should know; she lived it. Her faith was tested as never before at Ravensbruck—Betsie's too—and they prevailed.

Corrie wrote a book about her experiences called *The Hiding Place*, which later was made into a fine motion picture. As I said, I had the blessed privilege of sharing lunch with this extraordinary woman. She was 87 at the time and still going strong for the Lord. During the meal I asked her, "Miss ten Boom, if you could tell a young man something to help him, what would you tell me?"

Her answer changed my life. "Myles," she said, "just remember to grow where you are planted." That's what I have done ever since. I established Bahamas Faith Ministries in 1980, and nearly 30 years later I'm still here. People come and go, which is normal, but I'm still here. And some of the people laboring with me at BFM have been here from the beginning. Grow where you are planted. Bloom wherever God has placed you. Through the years at BFM we have endured all sorts of storms, persecution, and trials. Why? Because we are planted. We are not here because things go well or poorly for us. We are here because God planted us. Grow where you are planted. Paul commended the Thessalonians: "...*among God's churches we boast about your perseverance and faith in all the persecutions and trials you are enduring*" (2 Thess. 1:4). Think about the trials you have faced in the past, or the ones you may be going through now. Would Paul boast about *your* perseverance and faith? More importantly would God?

Paul also said that when our faith stands up to testing, we are "counted worthy of the kingdom of God" (2 Thess. 1:5b). Our worthiness for God's Kingdom is tied to our ability to endure hardship, to persevere under trials. With this in mind, we should welcome tests when they come, not because the tests are fun—they usually are not—but because we know that they are helping us grow to maturity and the fullness of Kingdom life. James, the half-brother of Jesus, put it this way:

> *Consider it pure joy, my brothers, whenever you*
> *face trials of many kinds, because you know that*
> *the testing of your faith develops perseverance.*
> *Perseverance must finish its work so that you may be*
> *mature and complete, not lacking anything*
> (James 1:2-4).

Every time you go through a period of hardship, strength and maturity are being developed in you. In other words, your circumstance is losing, and you are winning in the process. We rarely grow in good times. You can tell when God is ready for another jump in your life by the tests He allows to come your way. He takes you through a little tough period because He's getting ready to raise you to another level. So stand up to whatever life tosses your way, face it in faith, and come out victorious and stronger on the other side. Imagine what people will be able to say about you, and even better, about the God who strengthens you.

People around you are watching to see what kind of faith you have and what kind of God you serve. If all you have are "good" stories to tell, then they may conclude that God is nothing more than a celestial Santa Claus. But when they watch you go through hell and come out smiling and with no scent of smoke, they will say, "I want that kind of God." It is not what we escape, but what we endure that gains us respect with both a watching world and the Kingdom of God.

Biblical Heroes of Faith Who Passed the Test

If you are wondering whether you have what it takes to be a person of strong faith, or whether your questionable past may disqualify you, consider these biblical figures who passed the test. They were ordinary people like you and me, and with the exception of one (Jesus) they all failed in one way or another—some spectacularly—yet went on to victory, proving their worthiness for the Kingdom of God.

Moses killed an Egyptian. Moses murdered a man in cold blood when he saw him beating a Hebrew, one of his own people. In consequence, Moses had to flee for his life and spent the next 40 years in the desert raising sheep. Moses was God's chosen deliverer of the Israelites from Egyptian slavery. Was Moses' rash action a setback for God's plan? Perhaps, but it was nothing that took God by surprise. And Moses' 40 years in exile served to build his character and maturity so that when he returned to Egypt he was prepared for the task God had called him to do. Moses passed the test.

Abraham slept with his wife's handmaid. God had promised Abraham a son by his wife Sarah, but after many years of waiting, they decided to "help God." Sarah's handmaid, Hagar, became pregnant by Abraham and gave him a son, Ishmael. Yet God renewed His promise to Abraham for a son by Sarah, and Abraham believed God. When Abraham was 100 and Sarah 90, Sarah gave birth to Isaac. Abraham passed the test.

Joshua had to face Jericho. How could anyone succeed Moses? Yet that is just the challenge that Joshua faced. In order to encourage

Joshua, God promised to be with him and lead him and the people of Israel to victory. Shortly after Moses died, Joshua led the people across the Jordan River into the land of Canaan. God miraculously parted the waters of the river, just as He had done at the Red Sea for Moses, so the people could cross on dry ground. Sometimes God works a miracle to encourage us to keep going. Think of that as a bonus. More often than not, we have to fight the fight of faith. Joshua and the Israelites crossed the Jordan with confidence, worshiping and praising God. As soon as they reached the other side, they had to face the walled city of Jericho. Joshua may have thought they were going to get some rest, but God led them straight from one test into another. We can come through every test God allows to come our way and guess what? There will be another test up ahead. So if you keep trying to run away from tests, you will be running for the rest of your life. Joshua believed God, and the walls of Jericho fell. Joshua passed the test.

Daniel spent a night in a lion's den. Daniel was a man of God who believed in God, had faith in God, and obeyed God even at the threat of death from a pagan king. Yet he went into the lions' den and came out alive, healthy, and with no teeth marks. Our faith doesn't protect us *from* tests; it takes us *into* them. God wants to prove that the faith He gave us through His Word is stronger than any circumstances that can come against us. Being a Kingdom citizen does not give us immunity from tests and trials. As a matter of fact, Kingdom citizenship increases tests and trials, to prove that what we have is pure gold. Daniel passed the test.

David committed adultery with Bathsheba, and had her husband, Uriah, one of his best generals, killed in an effort to cover up his sin. Yet the Bible says that David was a man after God's own heart. Why? Because despite his great flaws, David also had many strengths; one of those strengths was that he loved God with all his heart. When confronted with his sin, David confessed, repented, and received God's forgiveness. In balance, David's life was one of faith, integrity, and righteousness. David passed the test.

Job lost everything. God allowed satan to test Job because satan insisted that Job's faith would last only as long as God continued to bless him. God knew better so He allowed satan to take away everything Job had. While Job maintained his claim of righteousness and openly questioned why he was made to suffer, he never once cursed God or abandoned his faith. In the end, God gave him back twice as much as he had had in the beginning. Job passed the test.

Jesus was betrayed by one of his best friends. It is always the people closest to us who hurt us the most. You cannot betray someone who doesn't trust you. Betrayal is possible only when trust is involved. Judas, one of Jesus' twelve disciples and closest followers, betrayed Him to His enemies. Did Jesus quit? No. But Judas committed suicide. Jesus even predicted he would do it. Shouldn't Jesus have felt guilty? No. Jesus said to Judas, in effect, "Do whatever you will. I'm not taking responsibility for your decision." And He kept on going. You may lose the best friend in your life, but you've got to get up and keep going. Jesus passed the test.

Paul was responsible for the deaths of many followers of Christ. Before becoming a believer himself, Paul passionately sought to stamp out the message of Christ and everyone who believed it. Yet God touched Paul and called Paul to be a missionary, and in response to that call Paul became, next to Christ Himself, the greatest force for the Gospel of Christ in history. Paul passed the test.

Peter denied Jesus. Even though he rashly promised that he wouldn't, when the test came, Peter gave in to fear and denied knowing Jesus. After His resurrection, Jesus restored Peter, and he never denied his Lord again. From then until the end of his life, Peter boldly proclaimed Christ, even dying because of his faith in Christ. Peter passed the test.

John was exiled on the island of Patmos. The last of the original twelve apostles of Jesus, John was exiled to Patmos by the Roman emperor because of his faith and testimony for Christ. While worshiping there one Lord's Day, John received a series of divinely inspired visions that became the Book of Revelation. John passed the test.

Our faith is qualified through tests. Paul says we become worthy of the Kingdom through persecution, perseverance, trials, and tests. So do well on your tests and give God a reason to put you on display. Don't believe God because of what He does for you, and don't put God down because of what He didn't do for you. Believe God because of who He is to you.

Fighting the Good Fight

In his first letter to Timothy, the apostle Paul encouraged the young man with these words:

> But you, man of God, flee from all this [the love of
> money], and pursue righteousness, godliness, faith,
> love, endurance, and gentleness. Fight the good fight
> of faith. Take hold of the eternal life to which you were
> called when you made your good confession in the
> presence of many witnesses (1 Timothy 6:11-12).

As we saw earlier, our fight is not a fight against the devil; our fight is for faith. The devil is fighting something else. He is attacking our belief system. If satan can get us to stop believing, to stop trusting in God, he has won. If you allow satan to tamper with your belief system he will destroy your life. That's why Paul says, *"Fight the good fight of faith."* In Romans 10:17 he says, *"Faith comes from hearing the message, and the message is heard through the word of Christ."* Faith is where the real fight is.

The desire to live a life of faith guarantees that tests and trials will come. Kingdom faith is both public and private. It is private in the sense that it involves for each of us our personal love relationship with God. It is public in the sense that we confess our faith publicly before others and go "on record" as believers. Paul urged Timothy to "take hold of the eternal life to which you were called when you *made your good confession in the presence of many witnesses."* Timothy's faith in Christ was a matter of public record. He was on the spot as a man of faith, and his faith was sure to be tested.

Anytime we make a public confession of our faith, we position ourselves for testing. God will allow our confession to be tested so that we ourselves, as well as the rest of the world, will know the genuineness of our faith. If you confess how good God has been to your business, get ready for a test to come with regard to your business. Some challenge, some setback, some reversal may come, and God is urging you, "Keep on believing. Don't quit just because things are a little tough. You trust Me when things are good. Trust Me now during the hard times. Hold fast to the confession you made in public."

You believe and testify that God will supply all your needs. What if He doesn't, and your money runs out? Can you keep on believing? Can you put up with an empty purse for a little while and never lose your confidence in God's faithfulness and provision? Can you look at your situation confidently as an opportunity to rise to the challenge of the test? Can you still turn on the stove and put on an empty pot believing that God will fill it somehow? Exercise your faith, and everything will be fine. Spend your Kingdom currency, and you will be all right. The Lord will bring you through. The God we serve is not

God only of the good times but of the bad times as well. So when you make confession before people, get ready for the test. *Faith confession will always attract the test of that faith.*

Believe Until You Win

Paul learned from firsthand experience how to contend for his faith. Toward the end of his life he was able to declare to Timothy:

> *I have fought the good fight, I have finished the race, I have kept the faith. Now there is in store for me the crown of righteousness, which the Lord, the righteous Judge, will award to me on that day—and not only to me, but also to all who have longed for His appearing* (2 Timothy 4:7-8).

Faith is a fight to finish and a race to run with a great award—the crown of righteousness—waiting at the end for all who pass the test. The race is to believe to the end, and the fight is to believe until you win. My friends, listen to me. It is not about how big you talk today. The question is, will you still be believing ten years from now? Can you endure the challenges, trials, and hardships that make you worthy of the Kingdom of God and still keep a positive attitude?

A complaining citizen is an immature citizen. Maturity means being willing to accept the bad along with the good, knowing that the bad can toughen us and make us better. The popular saying, "no pain, no gain," certainly is true of the Kingdom of God. So is the phrase, "no trials, no crown." This doesn't mean we have to go through trials in order to get to Heaven. The word *crown* has to do with rewards, not salvation. Our fitness to work and rule in the Kingdom of God as His co-regents is determined largely by the proving of our faith, by the tests we survive. *This is a Kingdom principle: the more you overcome, the more you will rule over. Perseverance under pressure prepares you for promotion.*

As believers we are all kings and queens destined for dominion, but in order to wear our crowns we have to go through some times of testing. So whenever you face trials, just remind yourself, "I'm working on my crown!" *I am expanding the size of my rulership domain.* Stand firm and the King Himself will place that crown upon your head as an award for your faithfulness. A *reward* is what you receive when you do something; an *award* is what you receive when you finish something. Run the race, finish the course, fight the good fight and never give up, and you will be awarded the crown of righteousness.

Learn to welcome tough circumstances as dear friends that have arrived to make you better and prepare you for your award. James tells us to look at trials that way, and so does Peter:

> *Praise be to the God and Father of our Lord Jesus*
> *Christ! In His great mercy He has given us new birth*
> *into a living hope through the resurrection of Jesus*
> *Christ from the dead, and into an inheritance that can*
> *never perish, spoil or fade—kept in heaven for you,*
> *who through faith are shielded by God's power until*
> *the coming of the salvation that is ready to be revealed*
> *in the last time. In this you greatly rejoice, though now*
> *for a little while you may have had to suffer grief in all*
> *kinds of trials. These have come so that your faith—of*
> *greater worth than gold, which perishes even though*
> *refined by fire—may be proved genuine and may*
> *result in praise, glory and honor when Jesus Christ is*
> *revealed* (1 Peter 1:3-7).

Trials endured purify our faith. They burn away the dross—the false, petty, and misguided thoughts, ideas, and beliefs that so easily become attached to our faith in the daily course of life. There is something about trials that clears our vision so that we can see what is truly important in life. They help us reorient our priorities. They help us remember that things are only things and never last anyway. Only that which is of Heaven will last, and that is where our focus needs to be.

Trials are the common lot of humankind. We all face them, and we cannot escape them, so the best thing we can do is let them work in our favor to build in us character and maturity. We have to fight the good fight of faith. We have to make it to the end. We have to overcome every circumstance. Our reward is waiting but we have to work for it. We have to endure the tests. Victory will come, but usually not right away. A delayed answer is still an answer; a delayed victory is still a victory.

That is the point Jesus was making in His story about a widow and an unjust judge.

> *Then Jesus told His disciples a parable to show them that they should always pray and not give up. He said: "In a certain town there was a judge who neither feared God nor cared about men. And there was a widow in that town who kept coming to him with the plea, 'Grant me justice against my adversary.'*
>
> *For some time he refused. But finally he said to himself, 'Even though I don't fear God or care about men, yet because this widow keeps bothering me, I will see that she gets justice, so that she won't eventually wear me out with her coming!'"*

*And the Lord said, "Listen to what the unjust judge
says. And will not God bring about justice for His
chosen ones, who cry out to Him day and night? Will
He keep putting them off? I tell you, He will see that
they get justice, and quickly. However, when the Son of
Man comes, will He find faith on the earth?"*
(Luke 18:1-8)

Do you ever feel like God is putting you off? I do. But I have learned over the years to trust that when God delays His answer, it is either because He is waiting for the right time, or because He has something better in store than what I asked for. Sometimes it is both. All of us know the feeling of longing and frustration that come in knowing what we desire and seeing it just beyond our reach. Or we pray and wonder why the pressure doesn't let up. Then we find ourselves asking, "Lord, why are You taking so long to bring this about?" That's when we need to remember that we work for Him; He is in charge, and He knows exactly what He is doing. He will not delay forever, and when His answer comes, we will understand that it came at exactly the right time and in just the right way to bring us to maturity and to bring glory to His name.

Many believers are always seeking "breakthroughs." They get depressed and go to a "breakthrough conference." They want to lick a problem in their life and start reading breakthrough books. And all the time there may be nothing for them to break through except their blood pressure. Most of the time our breakthroughs come as the result of steady, persistent, persevering faith, facing down the tests and trials of life as they come. All the while our faith and maturity grow until one day we suddenly realize that the breakthrough we sought so passionately long ago has come so gradually that we did not even notice it.

If God seems to be delaying something in your life, don't fret over it; just keep on trusting Him. He may be trying to develop your faith by holding off what you desire long enough for you to mature in that area. Then when He sees in you the faith and maturity He's looking for, He says, "OK, now you can have it."

Trials and tests are part of the daily life of a Kingdom citizen. Anyone who teaches or believes otherwise contradicts the Word of God. Still, it is amazing how many people leave the church or abandon the faith because they have been taught that children of God never have trials—that they are never broke, that they are never sick, that life is easy and trouble-free—but have found daily reality to be quite different. The message of trouble-free living for Christians is a lie. Kingdom faith is not faith that escapes trials, but faith that is built by, endures, and overcomes trials. Kingdom faith is tested faith, because the only way to build and strengthen true faith is through testing.

It is the tests we survive that make us worthy of the Kingdom of God. Luke 18:8 promises that God will see to it that we get justice and get it quickly. Quickly doesn't necessarily mean today or tomorrow morning. Quickly means when the time is right. When the right time arrives, BAM! Breakthrough will come overnight. Real breakthrough is when God's timing comes and we are not even expecting it. We pray for six weeks or six months or six years, and then all of a sudden God brings it about in six minutes. That's the way God works. His timing may not always be our timing, but His timing is never late.

Jesus' question is an important one for us today: *"When the Son of Man comes, will He find faith on the earth?"* Faith is what He is looking for. Not a big house or a fancy car or a lot of money in the bank, but faith. Not people who are always after miracles, signs, and wonders, but people of faith.

The fight is worth fighting and the race is worth running, because the end reward is great. As the writer of Hebrews tells us:

> *Therefore, since we are surrounded by such a great cloud of witnesses, let us throw off everything that hinders and the sin that so easily entangles, and let us run with perseverance the race marked out for us. Let us fix our eyes on Jesus, the author and perfecter of our faith, who for the joy set before Him endured the cross, scorning its shame, and sat down at the right hand of the throne of God. Consider Him who endured such opposition from sinful men, so that you will not grow weary and lose heart (Hebrews 12:1-3).*

Victory is in the air. Breakthrough is coming. Kingdom faith is tested faith. So run the race; finish the course; fight the good fight of faith. And remember, the race is to believe to the end, and the fight is to believe until you win.

Kingdom Principles

The key to effective living is the capacity and ability to manage the expected and the unexpected.

Success is measured by your ability to maintain personal balance in times of turmoil.

Maturity is measured by your capacity to respond effectively to tragedy and chaos.

Your faith is qualified through tests.

Faith confession will always attract the test of that faith.

*The more you overcome, the more you will rule over;
perseverance under pressure prepares you for promotion.*

Endnote

1. See http://www.corrietenboom.com/history.htm.

THE TEN QUALITIES OF KINGDOM FAITH

"Faith is a bird that feels dawn breaking and sings while it is still dark."
—Scandinavian saying

Like any other country, the Kingdom of Heaven functions by certain laws. Central to these is the law of faith. The Kingdom of God functions by faith, and without faith nothing functions in the Kingdom. We have already seen that faith is the culture and lifestyle of the Kingdom; it is also the currency of Kingdom economy. Successful Kingdom living is to live by faith not by sight, to trust totally in God rather than in our own wisdom.

Man was created to live by faith. Genesis 1:26 says that God created man in His own image and likeness. Image means nature or character. Man was created to be like God in character and nature. He was also created in God's likeness. Likeness does not have to do with appearance as much as with function. To be created in God's likeness means that man was created to function like God. And God functions by faith because He is a God of faith. So we are supposed to function by faith as well.

In the beginning Adam and Eve lived by what they believed, not by what they saw. That changed when they disobeyed God and ate fruit from the forbidden tree of the knowledge of good and evil. Their eyes were opened to the nature of evil, but their faith capacity diminished. Faith was no longer natural to them, and every succeeding generation of humankind has inherited that diminished capacity. Kingdom faith is not natural for us. Apart from the Spirit of God working in our lives, we cannot attain Kingdom faith, and without Kingdom faith, we will never see the Kingdom of God. Hebrews 11:6 says, *"And without faith it is impossible to please God, because anyone who comes to Him must believe that He exists and that He rewards those who earnestly seek Him."*

Anytime we try to function in an environment or manner different from that for which we were created, we end up being dysfunctional. In some cases it will even kill us. For example, if you try to function underwater for very long without some sort of breathing apparatus, you will die. Fish are designed to live in water; we are not. We were designed to live in an environment of faith, and outside that environment we cannot function properly.

The absence of faith creates a vacuum that is quickly filled, as you read earlier, by fear and doubt. Fear and doubt lead to worry, which is the antithesis of faith. There is nothing in our bodies that is designed to handle worry. In fact, scientific research has demonstrated that worry activates enzymes that cause our arteries and veins to constrict, thus restricting blood flow, which can lead to headaches, heart attack, stroke, and other cardiovascular ailments. So if you ever say, "I'm worrying myself to death," you are not exaggerating. God created you to function by faith, which means that unless you are functioning by faith, you are self-destructing. Without faith, you kick into worry, fretting, and mental depression, which eventually sabotages your life. You were designed to live by faith.

Faith supplants worry. It gives us access to the very things that we worry about not having: provision for our daily needs and confident hope for the future. This was Jesus' point when He said,

> So do not worry, saying, "What shall we eat?" or
> "What shall we drink?" or "What shall we wear?"
> For the pagans run after all these things, and your
> heavenly Father knows that you need them. But seek
> first His kingdom and His righteousness, and all these
> things will be given to you as well (Matthew 6:31-33).

In other words, Jesus is saying, "Don't preoccupy yourself with the daily needs of life. The King, your heavenly Father, will take care of those. Instead, preoccupy yourself with the things of the Kingdom of God. That is what you were designed for."

Living by Faith

Living by faith means living not by what your eyes show you but by what your mind, heart, and spirit know to be true. It is as you read earlier, "being sure of what we hope for and certain of what we do not see" (Heb. 11:1). Kingdom faith is a lifestyle of righteousness based on the nature and character of God. Righteousness means to be in right standing with God and in full compliance with the principles and laws of His government. From start to finish God's righteousness is imparted to us through faith: "For in the gospel a righteousness from God is revealed, a righteousness that is by faith from first to last, just as it is written: 'The righteous will live by faith'" (Rom. 1:17).

We have to believe that we are in right standing with God. Since we have no physical "proof," we must simply take God at His Word. If He says, "Your sins are forgiven through the blood of Jesus," we have to believe Him. And when we do, our hearts are filled with a confidence and sense of well-being that cannot be explained apart from the work of God's Spirit. The moment we first acknowledge Jesus Christ as our Savior and Lord, God imparts His righteousness to us, and it becomes an accomplished fact. From then on, through the rest of this life and into eternity, we live by faith and enjoy righteousness by faith.

As I mentioned in Chapter One, Kingdom faith means being willing to live with uncertainties and unknowns—the mysteries of life. Paul said, "*We live by faith, not by sight*" (2 Cor. 5:7). It is dangerous to stake our lives on what we see because so often what we see is not the complete picture. Looks can be deceiving unless we are viewing our situation from Heaven's viewpoint. Our physical eyes can play tricks on us, which is why we need to look at things through the spiritual eyes of faith. Living by sight binds our life to the whims of fate and circumstance, which can change with the wind. That kind of life has no stability. Living by faith on the other hand anchors your life on the unchanging truth of God, a foundation that will never be shaken.

Faith as the key to life is a common theme throughout the Scriptures. Genesis 15:6 says, "*Abram believed the Lord, and He credited it to him as righteousness.*" The Israelite people, after experiencing their miraculous deliverance from slavery in Egypt, as well as God's provision of food and water in the desert, refused to obey His command to cross the Jordan River and take the land of Canaan that He had promised to them. Instead of placing their faith in God, they chose to believe what they saw: an enemy that seemed too powerful for them to defeat. As a result of their faithlessness, God condemned them to wander in the desert for 40 years until that entire rebellious generation died. Over and over the Old Testament issues the call to believe, to trust, and to obey the Lord. David wrote, "*Some trust in chariots and some in horses, but we trust in the name of the Lord our God"* (Ps. 20:7).

The same emphasis is found in the New Testament. Jesus said, "Everything is possible for him who believes" (Mark 9:23b). The importance of living by faith was a constant theme in Paul's letters to the churches: *"For in the gospel a righteousness from God is revealed, a righteousness that is by faith from first to last, just as it is written: 'The righteous will live by faith'"* (Rom. 1:17). *"We live by faith, not by sight"* (2 Cor. 5:7). *"Clearly no one is justified before God by the law, because, 'The righteous will live by faith.' The law is not based on faith; on the contrary, 'The man who does these things will live by them'"* (Gal. 3:11-12).

The righteous will live by faith. Not by circumstances, or blessings, or prophecies, or miracles, or healings, or any other *thing*—but by faith alone. Don't let anything or anyone else become the source of your faith; because if you do, whenever they fail (and they will), your faith will also fail. So don't let whatever happens or doesn't happen in your life affect your faith in God. If you are a righteous Kingdom citizen you are supposed to live by faith. That means not backing off or giving up just because a little pressure or hardship comes along. "Shrinking violets" in the faith do not please the Lord: *" 'But My righteous one will live by faith. And if he shrinks back, I will not be pleased with him.' But we are not of those who shrink back and are destroyed, but of those who believe and are saved"* (Heb. 10:38-39).

Faith is the distinctive characteristic of the Kingdom of God and its citizens, and should set us apart from all other people on earth. God doesn't want children who shrink back in the face of difficulty or challenge. He wants children who stand in the middle of the storm, handle all earthquakes, and come through the fire without smelling of smoke, saying, "I made it through! Why? Because my God is an awesome God!" Faith that fails when trouble comes along is not really faith at all. True faith—Kingdom faith—believes in spite of trouble. It doesn't shrink back in the face of crisis or challenge. It doesn't surrender to persecution or waver under pressure. Kingdom faith overcomes in the face of trials and tribulations. Those whose faith fails are in danger of being destroyed. Faith is our protection against destruction.

Years ago when I was a student at ORU, Oral Roberts, who was president of the university at the time, said something in chapel one day that I have never forgotten. "Remember this, students," he said, "always keep your peace. And how do you keep your peace? Expect the best and prepare for the worst." *Expect the best and prepare for the worst.* The only way to prepare for the worst is through faith because only faith can take us through the tough times. Of course, we need a positive attitude, too! We should expect God to do great things and to bless us, but also be prepared to stand under whatever storms He allows to come. Faith will sustain us through the storms.

On the night He was betrayed, Jesus said to Simon Peter, "*Simon, Simon, Satan has asked to sift you as wheat. But I have prayed for you, Simon, that your faith may not fail. And when you have turned back, strengthen your brothers*" (Luke 22:31-32). Within hours Peter would deny His Lord three times, even after vowing that he would not. Peter failed that particular test, but his faith survived. His failure was due to relying too much on his own strength. As far as we know from Scripture, Peter never made that mistake again. He learned to anchor his faith not in his own capabilities, but in God. Jesus prayed for Peter's faith, which was the only thing that would see Peter through to the end.

Living by faith means not trusting in people or programs, but in God alone. It also means looking beyond sight to spiritual truth that usually is not visible to physical eyes. When Jesus first appeared to

His disciples after His resurrection, Thomas was not with them. When the others told him of it, Thomas insisted he would not believe unless he saw it with his own eyes. One week later he got his chance.

> A week later His disciples were in the house again, and Thomas was with them. Though the doors were locked, Jesus came and stood among them and said, "Peace be with you!" Then He said to Thomas, "Put your finger here; see My hands. Reach out your hand and put it into My side. Stop doubting and believe."
>
> Thomas said to Him, "My Lord and my God!"
>
> Then Jesus told him, "Because you have seen Me, you have believed; blessed are those who have not seen and yet have believed" (John 20:26-29).

How many of us have been like Thomas and said something like, "Until I see the miracle, I won't believe God"? To us, as to Thomas, Jesus says, "*Stop doubting and believe.*" Don't build your faith on what God shows you; build it on God, period. That's Kingdom faith.

Ten Essential Qualities of Kingdom Faith

By way of review, I want to discuss briefly ten essential qualities that characterize Kingdom faith, illustrating them with insights from Job, the Book of Hebrews, and Simon Peter.

1. Kingdom Faith Is Steadfast and Stable in Storms.

Job could be called the "poster child" for faith under pressure. When satan accused Job of trusting God for selfish reasons, God allowed satan to test Job's faith by stripping away everything he had.

Job lost his family, his wealth, and his health, but he never lost his faith in God. He wanted to question God as to the reason for his suffering, but he never turned his back on Him. Even when Job's three friends, assuming that Job's troubles were evidence of God's judgment against him, insisted that he confess his sins, Job maintained his faith, as well as his innocence:

> As surely as God lives, who has denied me justice, the Almighty, who has made me taste bitterness of soul, as long as I have life within me, the breath of God in my nostrils, my lips will not speak wickedness, and my tongue will utter no deceit. I will never admit you [Job's friends] are in the right; till I die, I will not deny my integrity. I will maintain my righteousness [his right standing with God] and never let go of it; my conscience will not reproach me as long as I live (Job 27:2-6).

Job did not understand why he was suffering or why God allowed it, but in the midst of the storm he kept on believing and kept on living the way he had always lived, with truthfulness, integrity, faithfulness, moral behavior, and a clear conscience. Because his faith was anchored in the living God, Job endured his period of testing without wavering. In good times as well as bad, Job trusted God as Lord of both. In fact, when challenged about his faith in the wake of losing everything, Job had countered, "Shall we accept good from God, and not trouble?" (Job 2:10a)

Like the house built on the rock that withstands the wind and the rain (see Matt. 7:24-25), Kingdom faith proves its foundation on the unshakeable God by remaining steadfast and stable through all the storms of life.

2. Kingdom Faith Is in God's Omniscient Knowledge, not Our Limited Knowledge.

The very existence of what we call "mysteries of life" proves that our knowledge is limited. Yet so often we talk and act as though we know everything. No matter what the circumstance, we tend to regard whatever we see with our eyes or perceive with our minds to be the full truth of the matter. Kingdom faith accepts with humility the reality of our limited knowledge and confidently leaves the rest in God's hands. This is something Job needed to be reminded of, for like most of us he got caught up in his pain and thought he knew more about the situation than God did. The Lord quickly set him straight:

> Then the Lord answered Job out of the storm. He said:
> "Who is this that darkens my counsel with words
> without knowledge? Brace yourself like a man; I will
> question you, and you shall answer me. Where were
> you when I laid the earth's foundation? Tell me, if
> you understand. Who marked off its dimensions?
> Surely you know! Who stretched a measuring line
> across it? On what were its footings set, or who laid its
> cornerstone—while the morning stars sang together
> and all the angels shouted for joy?" (Job 38:1-7)
>
> The Lord said to Job: "Will the one who contends with
> the Almighty correct Him? Let him who accuses God
> answer Him!" (Job 40:1-2)

Who among us could answer such questions? Job couldn't and neither can we. That's the whole point. God knows infinitely more than any of us will ever know. And He is under no obligation to explain either Himself or His actions to any of us. After all, who is accountable to whom? We are accountable to God, not vice versa. With Kingdom faith we accept our limited knowledge and are content to live with life's mysteries, trusting the unknown to God's omniscient knowledge, all-pervasive power, and perfect plan.

3. Kingdom Faith Is Beyond Our Own Understanding.

Because of our limited knowledge, there are some things that are, and always will be, beyond our understanding. Our human pride resists accepting this fact, which sometimes causes us to say and do some very stupid things. Some people believe that man is the measure of all things and that nothing, therefore, is ultimately beyond his understanding or capability. Our intellectual, scientific, and technological advances outstrip our moral conscience, leading us often to do something because we *can*, without sufficiently dealing with the question of whether or not we *should*. Embryonic stem cell research and human cloning research are just two examples. We could all benefit from a healthy dose of Job's faith-inspired humility when confronted with the awesomeness of God and His infinite wisdom and power:

> Then Job replied to the Lord: "I know that You can
> do all things; no plan of Yours can be thwarted.
> You asked, 'Who is this that obscures My counsel
> without knowledge?' Surely I spoke of things I did not
> understand, things too wonderful for me to know. You
> said, 'Listen now, and I will speak; I will question you,
> and you shall answer me.' My ears had heard of You
> but now my eyes have seen You. Therefore I despise
> myself and repent in dust and ashes" (Job 42:1-6).

When Job saw the Lord with his own eyes, he immediately saw himself as he really was, and he responded to this revelation with abject humility. The prophet Isaiah had a similar experience:

> In the year that King Uzziah died, I saw the Lord seated on a throne, high and exalted, and the train of His robe filled the temple. Above Him were seraphs, each with six wings: With two wings they covered their faces, with two they covered their feet, and with two they were flying. And they were calling to one another: "Holy, holy, holy is the Lord Almighty; the whole earth is full of His glory." At the sound of their voices the doorposts and thresholds shook and the temple was filled with smoke.
>
> "Woe to me!" I cried. "I am ruined! For I am a man of unclean lips, and I live among a people of unclean lips, and my eyes have seen the King, the Lord Almighty" (Isaiah 6:1-5).

Humility is the only appropriate response to a revelation of God in all His majesty. Kingdom faith acknowledges this and is willing to live with the fact that there are some things we will never understand. But God understands, and that is enough.

4. Kingdom Faith Is Rewarded After the Tests.

Job stood firm in his faith and in the knowledge of his righteousness not only in the face of his suffering but also in the face of the accusations from his three friends. Eliphaz, Bildad, and Zophar attributed Job's troubles to God's disfavor toward him. Because they misunderstood God, they also misrepresented Him. In the end, God vindicated Job and called his three friends to account:

> After the Lord had said these things to Job, he said to
> Eliphaz the Temanite, "I am angry with you and your
> two friends, because you have not spoken of Me what
> is right, as My servant Job has. So now take seven bulls
> and seven rams and go to My servant Job and sacrifice
> a burnt offering for yourselves. My servant Job will
> pray for you, and I will accept his prayer and not deal
> with you according to your folly. You have not spoken
> of Me what is right, as My servant Job has." So Eliphaz
> the Temanite, Bildad the Shuhite and Zophar the
> Naamathite did what the Lord told them; and the Lord
> accepted Job's prayer (Job 42:7-9).

Not only was Job right and his self-righteous friends wrong, God accepted Job's prayer on their behalf to forgive them for misrepresenting Him and to accept their sacrifices of repentance. As if this were not enough, God vindicated Job even further:

> After Job had prayed for his friends, the Lord made him
> prosperous again and gave him twice as much as he
> had before. All his brothers and sisters and everyone
> who had known him before came and ate with him in
> his house. They comforted and consoled him over all
> the trouble the Lord had brought upon him, and each
> one gave him a piece of silver and a gold ring
> (Job 42:10-11).

Because Job's faith stood firm throughout the test, he received God's reward at the end. He had lost everything he had, but God restored to him twice as much. In other words, Job was blessed before the test, but *doubly* blessed after the test. Kingdom faith always brings rewards, some in this life, but even more in the life to come.

5. Kingdom Faith Is Rewarded by the King.

Notice also that Job's reward came directly from God. In any kingdom one of the functions of the king is to bestow good things on his people, especially rewards for faithful service. In Job's case, his rewards show not only the beneficence and infinite resources of God, but also that when God blesses faithfulness, He never uses half-measures.

> *The Lord blessed the latter part of Job's life more than the first. He had fourteen thousand sheep, six thousand camels, a thousand yoke of oxen and a thousand donkeys. And he also had seven sons and three daughters....Nowhere in all the land were there found women as beautiful as Job's daughters, and their father granted them an inheritance along with their brothers.*
>
> *After this, Job lived a hundred and forty years; he saw his children and their children to the fourth generation. And so he died, old and full of years* (Job 42:12-13;15-17).

Here's another reason to remain faithful through the storm: if you give up and drop out in the midst of the test, you will miss out on the great rewards that follow. Consider Job's wife. In the beginning of Job's ordeal, right after he lost everything, his wife told him to "*curse God and die*" (Job 2:9b). Job rebuked her with the words, "*You are talking like a foolish woman. Shall we accept good from God and not trouble?*" (Job 2:10a). After this, nothing more is heard of Job's wife.

We can only assume that something happened to her. It is quite possible that she left Job. If so, then she missed out on the abundance of blessing that came to him at the end. Not only did Job receive twice as much as he had in the beginning, he also had seven children to replace the ones who died. This implies that Job also got another wife, one whose faith was more in line with his than that of his first wife. Of course, most of this is speculation, but the point is that loss of faith forfeits latter rewards. The King rewards generously, but He does not reward the faithless.

6. Kingdom Faith Is Given and Sustained by the King.

Many people assume that faith comes from the mind of man and is something we offer to God on our own initiative. While human free will certainly plays a part, faith itself originates with God. Paul wrote, *"For it is by grace you have been saved, through faith—and this not from yourselves, it is the gift of God—not by works, so that no one can boast. For we are God's workmanship, created in Christ Jesus to do good works, which God prepared in advance for us to do"* (Eph. 2:8-10).

Faith is the gift of God. Because of our sinful nature that rebels against God, we cannot generate true faith completely on our own. Jesus said, *"No one can come to Me unless the Father who sent Me draws him, and I will raise him up at the last day"* (John 6:44). Because faith is a gift of God, He draws us to Christ before we ever choose to come to Christ.

Not only does faith originate with God, but He also sustains it and brings it to completion, which is something else we could never do by ourselves. That is why the writer of Hebrews says, *"Let us fix our eyes on Jesus, the author and perfecter of our faith, who for the joy set before Him endured the cross, scorning its shame, and sat down at the right hand of the throne of God"* (Heb. 12:2).

The King gives faith to whomever He chooses, and without His gift no one ever comes to faith. Through God's gift of faith, we draw near to Christ and trust Him for the forgiveness of our sins and for new life in Him. Then through His Holy Spirit, He sustains and completes faith in us so that we endure every challenge and pass every test. From start to finish, faith is the work of the King.

7. Kingdom Faith Is Stronger than Blood.

When we become believers and followers of Christ, we are born into a new family, the family of God, with which our faith forms a bond stronger even than the blood ties of our earthly family. Jesus made this point repeatedly as a primary aspect of discipleship:

> *If anyone comes to Me and does not hate his father and mother, his wife and children, his brothers and sisters—yes, even his own life—he cannot be My disciple* (Luke 14:26).

> *Anyone who loves his father or mother more than Me is not worthy of Me; anyone who loves his son or daughter more than Me is not worthy of Me* (Matthew 10:37).

> *While Jesus was still talking to the crowd, His mother and brothers stood outside, wanting to speak to Him. Someone told Him, "Your mother and brothers are standing outside, wanting to speak to You."*

> *He replied to him, "Who is My mother, and who are My brothers?" Pointing to His disciples, He said, "Here are My mother and My brothers. For whoever does the will*

> *of My Father in heaven is My brother and sister and*
> *mother"* (Matthew 12:46-50).

> *"I tell you the truth,"* Jesus replied, *"no one who has*
> *left home or brothers or sisters or mother or father*
> *or children or fields for Me and the gospel will fail*
> *to receive a hundred times as much in this present*
> *age (homes, brothers, sisters, mothers, children and*
> *fields—and with them, persecutions) and in the age to*
> *come, eternal life* (Mark 10:29-30).

Kingdom faith is not only stronger than blood ties of family, it is also stronger than the fear of having one's own blood shed: *"Consider Him (Christ) who endured such opposition from sinful men, so that you will not grow weary and lose heart. In your struggle against sin, you have not yet resisted to the point of shedding your blood"* (Heb. 12:3-4). History is replete with examples of believers who were faithful under every sort of trial and persecution, even unto death. What about you? How far has your faith been tested?

8. Kingdom Faith Is Purified by Tests.

Faith cannot grow without being tested. Until it is proven in the crucible of life, faith is of little value. Kingdom faith is more than just words; it reveals itself in good works and proves itself in the endurance of trials. *Your faith is only as strong as the tests it survives.* Anyone whose faith consists of words only and is not backed up by lifestyle, has no faith at all. That is the sobering assessment of James, the brother of Jesus, who wrote,

> *What good is it, my brothers, if a man claims to have*
> *faith but has no deeds? Can such faith save him?*
> *Suppose a brother or sister is without clothes and daily*

food. If one of you says to him, "Go, I wish you well;
keep warm and well fed," but does nothing about his
physical needs, what good is it? In the same way, faith
by itself, if it is not accompanied by action, is dead.

But someone will say, "You have faith; I have deeds."
Show me your faith without deeds, and I will show you
my faith by what I do.…As the body without the spirit
is dead, so faith without deeds is dead
(James 2:14-18,26).

People possessing Kingdom faith welcome tests because they have come to understand that tests purify their faith and help them grow to maturity. Peter was one of several New Testament writers who emphasized this truth:

Praise be to the God and Father of our Lord Jesus
Christ! In His great mercy He has given us new birth
into a living hope through the resurrection of Jesus
Christ from the dead, and into an inheritance that can
never perish, spoil or fade—kept in heaven for you,
who through faith are shielded by God's power until
the coming of the salvation that is ready to be revealed
in the last time. In this you greatly rejoice, though now
for a little while you may have had to suffer grief in all
kinds of trials. These have come so that your faith—of
greater worth than gold, which perishes even though
refined by fire—may be proved genuine and may
result in praise, glory and honor when Jesus Christ is
revealed. Though you have not seen Him, you love
Him; and even though you do not see Him now, you

*believe in Him and are filled with an inexpressible and
glorious joy, for you are receiving the goal of your faith,
the salvation of your souls* (1 Peter 1:3-9).

The next time you face a test, remember that its purpose is to purify your faith and make you strong.

9. Kingdom Faith Does Not Fear Trials.

Much of our modern-day faith teaching would not stand up to the accounts in Scripture of the trials of the faith. Most of the faith of today's 21st-century believer is only good for receiving and expecting blessings and designed only to survive good times. Perhaps this is why many are quick to blame the devil for any form of discomfort and try to avoid the part of resistance.

However, because true Kingdom citizens recognize the purpose and value of tests for the maturing of their faith, they do not fear the tests. They have learned to experience the precious presence of the Lord with them during their trials, which gives them an entirely different perspective on what they are going through—a heavenly perspective. Peter encouraged the readers of his first letter with these words:

*Dear friends, do not be surprised at the painful trial
you are suffering, as though something strange were
happening to you. But rejoice that you participate in
the sufferings of Christ, so that you may be overjoyed
when His glory is revealed. If you are insulted because
of the name of Christ, you are blessed, for the Spirit of
glory and of God rests on you. If you suffer, it should
not be as a murderer or thief or any other kind of
criminal, or even as a meddler. However, if you suffer*

> *as a Christian, do not be ashamed, but praise God that*
> *you bear that name* (1 Peter 4:12-16).

Peter says that painful trials are common for believers. It is part of life for Kingdom citizens residing in a sinful, fallen world. Furthermore, Peter tells us to *rejoice* that we participate in the sufferings of Christ. Why? Because when we participate in His sufferings, we also will participate in His glory and rewards later. How can we rejoice in suffering? It is impossible from a human perspective. Only the heavenly perspective, seen through the eyes of faith, makes it possible.

10. Kingdom Faith Commits the Future to God.

Everyone is interested in the future. Who wouldn't like to know what's going to happen tomorrow or next week or next year so we could prepare for it—good or bad? Millions of dollars are spent every year on psychics and fortunetellers. Many people read their daily horoscope as faithfully as they do the business or sports news. From a biblical perspective, the only legitimate "foretellers" were the ancient prophets of Israel, and even they were never shown everything. God alone knows the future in its fullness, and He guards it closely, revealing a bit here or a bit there on a "need-to-know" basis to particular people He chooses at particular times and for particular situations.

Kingdom faith people don't get caught up in the common frenzy to figure out the future. Just as they are content to live with the mysteries of life, they also are content not to know what the future holds because they know who holds the future. They understand that the sufferings of this life are nothing in comparison to the glories of the life to come in the Kingdom of God. So they endure with patience. I think this is what Peter had in mind when he wrote, "*So then, those who suffer according to God's will should commit themselves to their faithful Creator and continue to do good*" (1 Pet. 4:19).

Kingdom faith people may not know the future, but they know their future is secure. By faith they have committed their future to God, the King, as citizens of His Kingdom, a Kingdom of infinite power, beauty, glory, and goodness that will stand forever.

Kingdom Principles

Kingdom faith is steadfast and stable in storms.

Kingdom faith is in God's omniscient knowledge, not our limited knowledge.

Kingdom faith is beyond our own understanding.

Kingdom faith is rewarded after the tests.

Kingdom faith is rewarded by the King.

Kingdom faith is given and sustained by the King.

Kingdom faith is stronger than blood.

Kingdom faith is purified by tests.

Kingdom faith does not fear trials.

Kingdom faith commits the future to God.

CHAPTER FIVE

LET GOD BE GOD

"Fear knocked at the door and faith answered. No one was there."
—*Old English Proverb*

Kingdom citizens walk by faith, not by sight, but this does not mean our faith is blind. On the contrary. Kingdom faith is not a leap in the dark, but a walk illuminated by the bright light of Heaven. *Kingdom faith is a confident leap in the bright light of God's faithfulness to His Word. Kingdom faith is not a vacillating belief in chance but a bold conviction in the credibility of the King and government of Heaven. Kingdom faith is faith in His faithfulness.*

When we walk by faith, we see from a heavenly perspective that is far more vast and all-encompassing than any view from the physical plane. Circumstances and realities that are invisible from the purely human standpoint are opened to our view because Kingdom faith, while not based on sight, *is* based on *vision*.

Through the eyes of faith we understand that *everyone was created to fulfill a purpose.* God has a reason for everything He does or allows, so the fact that you and I are here on this earth is no accident. If you are alive and breathing, God has a plan and a purpose for your life: " *'For I know the plans I have for you,' declares the Lord, 'plans to prosper you and not to harm you, plans to give you hope and a future'"* (Jer. 29:11). The word *hope* here does not refer to wishful thinking, but to a certainty based on the unshakeable integrity of God's promise, even if it is not yet visible. We can entrust our future to God because His Word is true, and because, as we walk by faith, He gives us vision related to His purpose for each of us.

Your purpose is your vision assignment for your life. And this vision is revealed through faith. Many people live their entire lives and never discover who they are or what they were meant to do. Kingdom life means being brought out of the darkness of unknowing into the light of purpose and relationship: *"But you are a chosen people, a royal priesthood, a holy nation, a people belonging to God, that you may declare the praises of Him who called you out of darkness into His wonderful light. Once you were not a people, but now you are the people of God; once you had not received mercy, but now you have received mercy"* (1 Pet. 2:9-10).

As Kingdom citizens and God's "chosen people," we are the royal children of the King. Children of earthly royalty are groomed from birth to know who they are, what they are to do, and how they are to behave as princes and princesses. God's Kingdom operates the same way. He gives you a vision of who you are and what He wants you to do, and that vision is your life assignment from your King and Father. Fulfilling that vision makes up your purpose in life. Kingdom faith helps you see and understand the vision from your Father. What vision has He given you?

Whatever your vision, one thing is certain: *every vision will be tested for authenticity.* No one is exempt from tests in life, and this is especially true for Kingdom citizens. Being born is the only necessary qualification. Generally speaking, the tests we face will relate to the vision we have received. So the safest way to avoid major tests in your life is to decide not to fulfill your vision. In other words, just decide not to be yourself, and you won't have too much trouble in life. Of course you also will end up being and doing nothing. But the moment you discover and decide to pursue your assignment, you set yourself up for tests.

Stop believing the lie that testing is a sign that you are out of God's will. Not at all. Testing is a sign that you are *in* His will! The devil doesn't bother trying to stop someone who isn't going anywhere anyway. Your vision assignment will be tested for authenticity. This means that God has designed life in such a way as to test you to see if what you claim God told you to do is authentic. So if you don't want to be tested greatly, do little things or do nothing. Remember: if you aim at nothing, you will always hit it. But what's the value in that? Anyone can fail in life. It takes determination and faith to succeed. Fulfillment in life means understanding your vision, rising to the challenge, pursuing your purpose, and welcoming the tests that come as opportunities to prove that your vision is authentic.

The test is not to destroy you but to prove your vision. You will never know who you really are until you are tested. God doesn't allow tests in your life because He wants to destroy you. He allows tests so that you can discover what you are made of, how thoroughly you trust God, and how deeply you believe in your own assignment.

Abraham was tested in just this way. God had promised Abraham a son in his old age by his barren wife Sarah. After waiting 25 years for fulfillment, Abraham finally saw the birth of Isaac, through whom God had promised to make of Abraham a mighty nation. Then when Isaac was still young, probably in his teens, God tested Abraham by commanding him to sacrifice Isaac to Him as a burnt offering. God never intended Abraham to follow through, but He was testing Abraham's faith. How far would Abraham go in his obedience to

God? The test was for Abraham's sake; God already knew the faith that was in Abraham's heart, but Abraham needed to know. Just before Abraham carried out the sacrifice of his son, God stopped him and provided a ram for Abraham to sacrifice. " 'Do not lay a hand on the boy,' He said. 'Do not do anything to him. Now I know that you fear God, because you have not withheld from Me your son, your only son' " (Gen. 22:12).

Abraham, already a man of great faith, came away from that experience with an even stronger faith, as well as a better understanding of God and the promise God had made to him. Abraham's vision was of a nation descended from him that would bless all the people of the world, and now he knew beyond doubt that God would bring it about. Abraham's test proved his vision and solidified his faith.

Your test probably won't be like Abraham's, but whatever form it takes, it will be just as significant in the life of your faith and in the proof of your vision. If God has given you a vision, He will test it. Don't dread the test— welcome it.

God Is God; We Are Not

How do we get it into our heads that we think we know better than God? Despite all the mistakes we make, no matter how often we mess up, and regardless of abundant evidence to the contrary, we persist in believing that somehow we can run our lives better than God can. Pride lies at the heart of this attitude, the same pride that got Adam and Eve in trouble in the Garden of Eden.

We must relax and learn to let God be God. He is God; we are not. Anything forced to function in a manner contrary to its design eventually malfunctions. If we try to play God, we will only wear ourselves out with frustration and failure. More than that, we may put our lives in danger, because God will brook no rivals. The only proper course—not to mention the safest—is to humbly accept our place as being created *"a little lower than God"* (Ps. 8:5 NASB) and allow God to be God. This means accepting our own limitations while acknowledging that God has none.

In Chapter One, we talked about knowing our limitations, knowing what we are and are not responsible for and what we can and cannot do. Now we are looking at the reverse side. First of all, *there are some things only God can do.* Only God can bring a physical universe into being out of nothing. The best we can do is to fashion something original out of material already at hand. Only God can create life. Scientists have sought to duplicate this in the laboratory by gathering together the "building blocks" of life and then trying to recreate the conditions they believe existed on earth millions of years ago, assuming that life would spring forth spontaneously. They have failed. Only God can change a human heart, transforming an angry rebel into a joyful child of God. Therapy may help a troubled person feel better about himself, but all the counseling and pop psychology in the world cannot alleviate the central problem: pride arising from a sinful heart. Only God can forgive sin. Only He can root it out at the source—the human heart—and excise it. There are some things only God can do.

There are some things only God knows. One of the most honest and most liberating things we can say to another person is, "I don't know." We are so afraid to admit our ignorance, so afraid that other people will think we are stupid. We have to be in control, or at least make others think we are. One of the reasons there is so much nonsense in the world is because so many people, and especially leaders and so-called "experts," will say anything to avoid damaging their reputations by being seen as—or thought to be—lacking in knowledge. Proverbs 1:7 says, *"The fear of the Lord is the beginning of knowledge, but fools despise wisdom and discipline."* In other words, the fear of the

Lord is the starting point of true knowledge. We do not know every-thing, and we cannot know everything. Part of "fearing" the Lord is acknowledging the fact that there are some things only God knows.

There are some things only God understands. We cannot possibly comprehend everything that happens in life. Some things simply defy our understanding. This is one reason why Kingdom faith is so important. Kingdom faith can help us be at peace and full of confi-dence in a world that often doesn't make sense. There comes a time when we have to say, "You know, God, I really don't understand this. But You do, and that's all I need to know." Are you perplexed or both-ered by all the things you do not understand? Surrender your lack of understanding to God's omniscience. Rest in the assurance that He has everything under control, including the things that don't make sense to you.

There are things only God can explain. One of the biggest hin-drances many believers face in growing a mature faith is their belief that they are entitled to an explanation for everything that God allows into their lives. As we saw in Chapter Four, God is under no obligation to explain either Himself or His actions to any of us. Job was tested as severely as anyone who has ever lived, and although he appealed repeatedly to God, he never learned *why* he was tested. When God finally spoke to Job, it was to challenge Job's presumption to debate life on God's level. While Job saw God as He was, recog-nized his own presumption, and repented *"in dust and ashes,"* (Job 42:6), God never revealed the reason for Job's trials. In the end, from Job's perspective, it didn't matter. He was content to let God be God, which means accepting the fact that there are some things only God can explain, and that He may not always choose to do so.

The upshot of all this is that *we have to know our limits.* We have to learn to change the things we can, accept with grace the things we cannot change, and be at peace with that balance. All things are possible with God. So when you face the undoable, the unknown, the incomprehensible, and the unexplainable, entrust them to the God of the impossible.

Designed for the Tests

Ultimately, faith is the only means we have for making sense of the world and finding meaning in life. Some things defy explanation and exceed our human capacity to understand. In those situations, all we have to go on is faith, but if our faith is in the living God and in the integrity of His Word, then faith is all we need. Faith creates confidence. *Lack of confidence is a symptom of lack of faith.* Armed with faith we can walk into the world with confidence every day, no matter how the environment looks. Faith gives us the sure conviction that we are going to win regardless of present circumstances. It also assures us of success in the tests we are sure to face.

Our faith is manifested by the tests it encounters. In other words, tests reveal the nature and quality of our faith—and even whether or not faith is present. As I've said before, our faith is only as strong as the tests it survives. This is why God allows our faith to be tested. He wants our faith not only to survive, but also to thrive, and that can occur only in an environment of testing. As a matter of fact, God *designed* us for testing. So tests are good for us, as long as they are the right kind of tests. We test ourselves over and over with the wrong things and then wonder why our lives are messed up. God's tests are engineered to suit our design and therefore serve to strengthen and prepare us for Kingdom use.

If you buy a car that has a speedometer that reads as high as 180 mph, the manufacturer of that car is certifying that it will handle 180 mph. Perhaps you have never driven that fast, and you certainly had no input into the calibration of the speedometer. How do you know the car will reach that velocity? What gives the manufacturer the right to make that claim?

Testing.

Automobile manufacturers maintain test tracks where they test new models and designs. A test track is like a race track. When a company designs a new engine, for example, it builds a prototype and then mounts that prototype into a test car. A test driver employed by the company then takes the test car onto the test track and puts the new engine through its paces. The engineers and company executives want to make sure the engine can perform to its design parameters. The test driver will stress the engine and press it to its maximum—180 mph, let's say—and keep it there for a certain period of time. If the prototype engine fails the test, they scrap it and start over. However, if it passes the test—if it performs as it was designed to perform—then the order goes out: "Replicate this engine; reproduce it in exact detail 300,000 times." They don't test every engine; they test one engine and then reproduce 300,000 in its image. Then the company can claim that every car with that engine can reach 180 mph. Why? Because the tested engine did it, and if the tested engine did it, then every engine made in its image and likeness should be able to do it also.

On the night before He died, Jesus told Peter, *"Simon, Simon, satan has asked to sift you as wheat. But I have prayed for you, Simon, that your faith may not fail. And when you have turned back, strengthen your brothers"* (Luke 22:31-32). Peter was about to be tested, and after the bitter sorrow and regret of his denial of Jesus, Peter's faith would be restored and strengthened as never before. Then, when he had passed the test, he could strengthen others.

If you are going through a tough time, it is a good sign that God wants to use you as a model. Pass your test. Stand firm through the difficulties you are facing because God wants to make a lot of people in your image. You may pray for God to take away the hardship in your life, but He may want you to believe Him *through* the hardship because He knows that there are some people watching you who need to see that your faith can handle all the stress and still come out smiling on the other side. Your faith under stress can strengthen and encourage *others* to stand firm as well.

A Way Out

The key to success in tests is faith seasoned with a healthy dose of humility. There is no faster way to fall than to become too proud of yourself for standing firm. Proverbs 16:18 says, *"Pride goes before destruction, a haughty spirit before a fall."* Paul reiterates this danger in his warning to the believers in Corinth: *"So, if you think you are standing firm, be careful that you don't fall!"* (1 Cor. 10:12). In other words, Paul is saying, if you think you are strong, watch out! If you think you have it all together, be careful! If you are prone to criticize or judge others for their mistakes and failings, don't do it because you may be next! Jesus said, *"Blessed are the merciful, for they will be shown mercy"* (Matt. 5:7). It is the law of reciprocation: if you want to receive mercy when you fall, be merciful to others who have fallen. No one is perfect. No one is so strong in faith as to be immune to temptation.

God realizes this, which is why He gives us a way out. As Paul explains: *"No temptation has seized you except what is common to man. And God is faithful; He will not let you be tempted beyond what you can bear. But when you are tempted, He will also provide a way out so that you can stand up under it"* (1 Cor. 10:13).

Do you think your troubles are unique? Do you think no one else has ever gone through what you're going through? Do you think you are special? Think again. Nobody's special. None of us can lay a claim to a one-of-a-kind problem that no one else has ever faced before. Your temptations and mine are those that are common to all people. Not even Jesus was immune. He spent 40 days fasting in the desert where He was tempted by the devil. He passed the test by keeping His focus in the right place: on His Father and on the mission His Father had given Him. This should encourage us. Because Jesus experienced temptation Himself, He knows what it's like. He understands what we are going through and extends mercy to us. This is what the writer of Hebrews had in mind when he wrote:

> Therefore, since we have a great high priest who has gone through the heavens, Jesus the Son of God, let us hold firmly to the faith we profess. For we do not have a high priest who is unable to sympathize with our weaknesses, but we have one who has been tempted in every way, just as we are—yet was without sin. Let us then approach the throne of grace with confidence, so that we may receive mercy and find grace to help us in our time of need (Hebrews 4:14-16).

Because Jesus understands what we're going through when we are tested, He can keep us strong in it so that when the next person goes through it, we can say from experience, "Hang in there! You're going to make it!" We can take courage from the fact that the Lord is faithful, even when we are not. He can (and will) see us through even when we fear we can't make it. Scripture says, "*The righteous cry out, and the Lord hears them; He delivers them from all their troubles…. A righteous man may have many troubles, but the Lord delivers him from them all*" (Ps. 34:17,19).

God is so faithful to His children, in fact, that He will not allow us to be tempted beyond what we can bear. Who knows what an engine can bear better than those who designed and built it? God created us; who knows what we can bear better than He? Even we ourselves, because of our limited vision and knowledge, do not know our full capabilities the way God does. If you are facing a challenge that seems insurmountable to you, just remember that God has promised that He will not allow you to be tested beyond that which you are able to overcome. In other words, no test will come your way that can destroy you; God will not allow it.

Notice, however, that God will not remove all tests and temptations from our path. To do that He would have to remove us from the world. Instead, He limits our tests to what we can bear and even then provides a "way out" so that we can "stand up under it." So whenever you face a trial, it is as if God is saying, "I know you can handle this, so handle it! Don't whine and don't complain. Be bold and courageous. Exercise your faith. Spend some of your Kingdom currency, and stand!" Your test is a sign of God's confidence in you. Stand firm, and He will make a way of escape.

God will provide a way out, but unless we are in tune with His Spirit, we may miss it. When trouble comes, we often make assumptions as to how and when God will deliver us. We expect Him to act in a predictable manner that we can understand. More often than not, however, God works in unexpected ways. Then when we don't see God move in the way we anticipated, we get confused, frustrated, and frightened, and may even conclude that He has let us down.

One reason for the confusion is that we tend to focus on our own needs and agenda while God is always acting with the bigger picture in view. He will deliver us, but in ways designed to serve His greater purpose and not just our own narrow interests. Daniel's way out was *through* the lions' den. Shadrach, Meshach, and Abednego's way out was *through* the fiery furnace. Paul and Silas had to go *through* beating and imprisonment in the Philippian jail before deliverance came by way of an earthquake. In each of these instances, deliverance came in a manner different from expected, but in the end God was glorified, and lives were changed.

Suppose you have a loved one who is very sick. You pray constantly asking God to heal this person. You bring elders from the church to anoint your loved one with oil and pray over him or her. You carry the sick one to healing crusades to receive special prayer and the laying on of hands. You do everything you know to do, and yet your loved one still dies. What now? Is God still God? Did He answer your prayers, or did He ignore you? Oral Roberts used to say that God heals in two ways: temporarily and permanently. In this case, He chose to heal permanently by taking your loved one home. He provided a way out, but in a manner different from what you hoped and expected.

So when you are tested, stand firm and look for God's way out, but be ready for it to appear in an unexpected manner or from an unanticipated direction. Let God be God.

Knowing Our Limits

Understanding that God acts in unexpected ways is another reason for openly acknowledging our limitations. As long as we insist that we should know everything or be able to do anything, we will be continually frustrated when God consistently fails to perform according to our plan. In reality, accepting our limitations is a very liberating experience. It is one of the key elements of Kingdom faith. As I said in Chapter Two, when in doubt, have faith; when you don't know what to do, believe; when nothing makes sense, trust. Knowing our limits frees us in ways that nothing else can. How? Because *Kingdom faith submits its limitations to the unlimited God.* In the hands of an unlimited God our limitations become strengths. Paul stated that God's power is made perfect in our weakness and then declared, *"That is why, for Christ's sake, I delight in weaknesses, in insults, in hardships, in persecutions, in difficulties. For when I am weak, then I am strong"* (2 Cor. 12:10).

Knowing our limitations forces us to rely on God's strength, wisdom, and power rather than our own. Peter thought he could stand up for Christ in his own strength, but suffered a humiliating failure when fear for his own safety led him to deny Christ three times. Once Peter acknowledged his weaknesses and submitted them to God, however, he became a powerhouse of faith, boldly proclaiming Christ before kings and emperors.

Trust your limitations to the unlimited God. Don't insist on trying to know everything. Whatever you need to know, He will teach you. Don't get frustrated because of the things you cannot do. Whatever you need to do—whatever God has called you to do—He will empower you to do. Let God be God. Let Him bring you along as He knows you are ready.

We would do well to consider again the words of David:

> My heart is not proud, O Lord, my eyes are not
> haughty; I do not concern myself with great matters
> or things too wonderful for me. But I have stilled and
> quieted my soul; like a weaned child with its mother,
> like a weaned child is my soul within me
> (Psalm 131:1-2).

Remember, these are the words of a king. David was the most powerful king of his day. Dozens of servants were at his beck and call. He could decide matters of life or death with a wave of his hand. Nothing that he desired would be denied him. Yet he was able to say, "*My heart is not proud.*" David remembered where he had come from. He never forgot that he was at heart a shepherd. David went on to say, "*My eyes are not haughty.*" The Hebrew word for *haughty* can mean "presumptuous;" it can also mean to look down on others with an air of superiority. Both attitudes are wrong. David did not presume to be more than he was. He was not a man to put on airs or regard himself as better than others simply because God had chosen him to be king.

Neither should we. Just because we are citizens of God's Kingdom and children of His royal family does not give us the right to look down our noses at others. Kingdom faith helps us stay in balance, and part of that balance comes in remembering not only who and where we are—children of God in His Kingdom of light—but also who we were and where we came from—slaves of sin, bound in satan's kingdom of darkness.

Next, David says, "*I do not concern myself with great matters or things too wonderful for me.*" As we saw before, there are some things that are too high for us; we cannot understand them. There are some things we are not supposed to know right now. God has His reasons and we need to trust Him. In a 1974 letter, Corrie ten Boom relates a memory from her childhood:

> I went to my father and said, "Daddy, I am afraid that I will never be strong enough to be a martyr for Jesus Christ." "Tell me," said Father, "When you take a train trip to Amsterdam, when do I give you the money for the ticket? Three weeks before?" "No, Daddy, you give me the money for the ticket just before we get on the train." "That is right," my father said, "and so it

is with God's strength. Our Father in Heaven knows when you will need the strength to be a martyr for Jesus Christ. He will supply all you need—just in time…"[1]

Kingdom faith is content to wait for God's "just in time." There are times we face situations and conditions in life when it feels like God does not care or is not aware of our predicament. There are times when God says nothing or seems to ignore our prayers. *Kingdom faith is confidence in the midst of God's silence.*

God Has Something Better

No matter how bright and beautiful our imaginings of the world and the life we dream of, God has something better in store. But sometimes we put so much stock in our own dreams that we cannot imagine anything better. Don't forget that our vision and knowledge are limited. We must see things from God's perspective in order to get the full picture. Isaiah 64:4 says, *"Since ancient times no one has heard, no ear has perceived, no eye has seen any God besides You, who acts on behalf of those who wait for Him."* Paul quoted this same verse in a slightly different form to the Corinthian believers: *"However, as it is written: 'No eye has seen, no ear has heard, no mind has conceived what God has prepared for those who love Him'"* (1 Cor. 2:9). The scope and beauty of what God has planned for us are beyond our comprehension. That is why Kingdom faith is so important; it teaches us to wait for God's best instead of settling for second best. If we are faithful, God will reveal His "something better" in His time and in His way.

This was the common testimony of the heroes of faith in the Bible, as the writer of Hebrews makes clear:

Now faith is being sure of what we hope for and
certain of what we do not see. This is what the ancients
were commended for (Hebrews 11:1-2).

The ancients were commended for their faith. A "roll call" of these faithful people follows as the writer cites them as positive examples: Abel, Enoch, Noah, Abraham, Isaac, Jacob, Moses, Rahab, Gideon, Barak, Samson, Jephthah, David, Samuel, and the prophets. Even though these people represent multiple generations, they shared at least one thing in common: faith in God that sustained them to live in the sure hope of His promises, even if they did not live to see them personally. Again, in the words of the writer of Hebrews:

All these people were still living by faith when they
died. They did not receive the things promised; they
only saw them and welcomed them from a distance.
And they admitted that they were aliens and strangers
on earth. People who say such things show that they
are looking for a country of their own. If they had been
thinking of the country they had left, they would have
had opportunity to return. Instead, they were longing
for a better country—a heavenly one. Therefore God
is not ashamed to be called their God, for He has
prepared a city for them....These were all commended
for their faith, yet none of them received what had
been promised. God had planned something better for
us so that only together with us would they be made
perfect (Hebrews 11:13-16;39-40).

Another common factor linking all of these people is that they each suffered hardship as part of the cost of their faithfulness. They were tested and survived. They stood firm in their faith through the storms and were still standing on the other side. For many of them, the ultimate cost of their faith was death. But their death simply ushered them into the fullness of eternal life, the sure hope upon which they had anchored their earthly lives.

We will never be known for the things we avoided. We will never be remembered for the tests we failed (unless all we do is fail). History does not recall the cowards, the people who fled in the face of crisis, the faceless unknowns who achieved nothing in life because they attempted nothing. No, history remembers the people who lived (and died) by their convictions, who stood unwavering against all odds because they believed that what they stood for was worth the test.

People will remember us for the way we stay cool under pressure, calm in the midst of chaos, and confident when surrounded by uncertainty. Only one thing can give us that kind of equilibrium in life—Kingdom faith. Faith to trust in God even when life does not make sense. Faith to be content with our unknowing. Faith to accept our limitations. Faith to believe, even in the middle of the storm, that God will reward us on the other end. Faith, regardless of the present, that the future is so beautiful and glorious that God will purify us through the storm so that we can enjoy it to the fullest. *Faith to let God be God.*

Kingdom Principles

Kingdom faith is a confident leap in the bright light of God's faithfulness to His Word.

Your purpose is your vision assignment for your life.

Testing is designed not to destroy you, but to prove your vision.

Our faith is manifested by the tests it encounters.

If you are going through a tough time, it is a good sign that God wants to use you as a model.

The key to success in tests is faith seasoned with a healthy dose of humility.

Kingdom faith submits its limitations to our unlimited God.

Kingdom faith is confidence in the midst of God's silence.

Endnote

1. See www.libertytothecaptives.net/ten_boom.html; accessed 01/13/2009.

CHAPTER SIX

THE COURAGE
OF KINGDOM FAITH

"Faith is not belief without proof, but trust without reservation."
—Elton Trueblood

Kingdom faith is courageous faith—faith that does not give up because it knows
that current circumstances do not represent the full or final reality. Throughout the Scriptures God calls His people to faith, often coupling it with a call to courage. *Courage is not the absence of fear. Courage is confidence and conviction in the face of fear. Courage is belief in life beyond the obstacle of fear.*

In the days immediately following the death of Moses, God instructed Joshua, Moses' designated successor, to prepare the people of Israel to cross the Jordan River and conquer the land of Canaan, the "Promised Land" that God had promised to Abraham and his descendants. Moses had led the people for 40 years with great skill and numerous demonstrations of God's power; those would be tough shoes to fill. Add to that challenge the fact that the Canaanite people the Israelites would face were powerful in war and well-established in the land. Joshua faced the doubly tough challenge of not only winning the trust and respect of the Israelites as Moses' successor, but also inspiring them to cross the Jordan and take the land, something that the previous generation had refused to do.

Fortunately Joshua was not alone in the task. God knew that Joshua could not do the job by himself. Joshua was shouldering responsibilities and facing challenges that could make any reasonable person back away. And God also knew that the people as a whole were easily discouraged and prone to balk in the face of danger. As leader of the people, Joshua needed courage, and the people needed to be able to draw courage from the example of their leader. So before initiating the campaign to conquer the land of Canaan, God appeared to Joshua just as He had to Moses:

> After the death of Moses the servant of the Lord, the
> Lord said to Joshua son of Nun, Moses' aide: "Moses
> My servant is dead. Now then, you and all these
> people, get ready to cross the Jordan River into the
> land I am about to give to them—to the Israelites.
> I will give you every place where you set your foot,
> as I promised Moses. Your territory will extend from
> the desert to Lebanon, and from the great river, the
> Euphrates—all the Hittite country—to the Great Sea
> on the west. No one will be able to stand up against
> you all the days of your life. As I was with Moses, so I
> will be with you; I will never leave you nor forsake you.

> "**Be strong and courageous,** because you will
> lead these people to inherit the land I swore to
> their forefathers to give them. **Be strong and very
> courageous.** Be careful to obey all the law My servant
> Moses gave you; do not turn from it to the right or
> to the left, that you may be successful wherever you

*go. Do not let this Book of the Law depart from your
mouth; meditate on it day and night, so that you may
be careful to do everything written in it. Then you will
be prosperous and successful. Have I not commanded
you?* **Be strong and courageous.** *Do not be terrified;
do not be discouraged, for the Lord your God will be
with you wherever you go"*
(Joshua 1:1-9, emphasis added).

Three times in these verses God tells Joshua to *"be strong and courageous."* And although the word *faith* does not appear anywhere in
the passage, it is strongly implied throughout. God gives Joshua his
assignment, assures Joshua of His presence, and promises victory in
the coming campaign. Then He tells Joshua to be strong and courageous. Strong and courageous in what? In believing God and in
carrying out His instructions. It always takes courage to do what God
says. Faith and courage go together.

Courage is important in faith because, as we have seen throughout this book, Kingdom faith is a life filled with tests, trials, and hardships, and we need courage to face these storms. Sometimes God
performs great and miraculous works to encourage our faith, but we
must be careful not to misplace our faith. The goal of God's works is
that we place our faith in Him, *not* in His works. In the Gospel of John,
the apostle sets forth seven specific miracles, or signs, that Jesus performed to reveal to His disciples who He was and to build their faith.

In the first of these signs, Jesus changed water to wine at a wedding feast in the village of Cana. Afterward, John explained the
purpose of this miracle: *"This, the first of His miraculous signs, Jesus
performed in Cana of Galilee. He thus revealed His glory, and His disciples* **put their faith in Him**" (John 2:11). Jesus' disciples put their faith

in Him, not in His miracle of turning water into wine, because as far as we know, Jesus never did that again. It was a one-time miracle.

God's underlying goal behind His works, miracles, and blessings is that we place our faith in Him, not in the works themselves. In other words, God sometimes does amazing things in our lives so that we will learn to trust Him. Instead, what we do so often is trust in what He *did*. Then when the luster of that sign or blessing fades, we run off to try to get another one. And all the while God is saying, "Trust Me. Stop running around seeking miracles, signs, and blessings, and *trust Me*." God rarely does the same thing the same way twice, or the same way for two different people. For example, even though Joshua was Moses' designated successor, God never did anything for Joshua in the same way He had for Moses. Yet our tendency is to expect God to do the same thing tomorrow that He did today, or to work in someone else's life the same way He did in ours. Anytime we try to put God into that kind of box we're going to be disappointed.

So don't put your faith in what God did for me or for someone else. Put your faith in God; then relax and let Him deal with and do for you in His own unique way.

Courage to Face the Trials

Kingdom citizens have always faced trials of various kinds; it is in our spiritual genes. Remember Jesus' words: "*In this world you will have trouble. But take heart! I have overcome the world*" (John 16:33); and Paul's straightforward declaration: "*Everyone who wants to live a godly life in Christ Jesus will be persecuted*" (2 Tim. 3:12). Paul certainly should know, since he experienced persecution from both sides, first as a persecutor of believers, and then after becoming a follower of Christ, as a faithful messenger of the Gospel of Christ. In fact, Paul was an active participant in the persecution of the first recorded person to die because of faith in Christ: a man named Stephen.

Stephen's story is found in the sixth and seventh chapters of the Book of Acts. He first appears as one of seven men the church in Jerusalem selected to oversee the daily distribution of food to the needy in the church. Described as a man *"full of faith and of the Holy Spirit"* (Acts 6:5), Stephen was also a powerful public witness for Christ, which quickly got him into trouble:

> *Now Stephen, a man full of God's grace and power,*
> *did great wonders and miraculous signs among the*
> *people. Opposition arose, however, from members of*
> *the Synagogue of the Freedmen (as it was called)—*
> *Jews of Cyrene and Alexandria as well as the provinces*
> *of Cilicia and Asia. These men began to argue with*
> *Stephen, but they could not stand up against his*
> *wisdom or the Spirit by whom he spoke.*
>
> *Then they secretly persuaded some men to say, "We*
> *have heard Stephen speak words of blasphemy*
> *against Moses and against God."*
>
> *So they stirred up the people and the elders and*
> *the teachers of the law. They seized Stephen and*
> *brought him before the Sanhedrin. They produced*
> *false witnesses, who testified, "This fellow never stops*
> *speaking against this holy place and against the law.*
> *For we have heard him say that this Jesus of Nazareth*
> *will destroy this place and change the customs Moses*
> *handed down to us."*

> All who were sitting in the Sanhedrin looked intently at
> Stephen, and they saw that his face was like the face of
> an angel (Acts 6:8-15).

Hauled before the Jewish supreme religious court and falsely accused of blasphemy (a capital offense), Stephen proceeds in Acts 7 to give a lengthy defense of Christ and the Gospel of the Kingdom that is so brilliant it leaves his accusers speechless with rage:

> When they heard this, they were furious and gnashed
> their teeth at him.
> But Stephen, full of the Holy Spirit, looked up to heaven
> and saw the glory of God, and Jesus standing at the
> right hand of God. "Look," he said, "I see heaven open
> and the Son of Man standing at the right hand of God."
>
> At this they covered their ears and, yelling at the top of
> their voices, they all rushed at him, dragged him out
> of the city and began to stone him. Meanwhile, the
> witnesses laid their clothes at the feet of a young man
> named Saul [Paul].
>
> While they were stoning him, Stephen prayed, "Lord
> Jesus, receive my spirit." Then he fell on his knees and
> cried out, "Lord, do not hold this sin against them."
> When he had said this, he fell asleep (Acts 7:54-60).

Stephen was chosen as a servant/leader in the church because he was a man "full of faith." You have to be full of faith to be chosen in the Body of Christ. *The Kingdom of Heaven and its agency the Church can't afford to have weak-willed citizens who run whenever pressure comes.*

Faith, not talent, will get you through the trials. Faith, not gifting, will help you stand when everything else is collapsing.

Notice, however, that Stephen's faith did not prevent his stoning. He stood firm in his faith, and it cost him his life. Stephen was the first disciple to be stoned and killed because of his testimony for Christ. When you face trials or hardship, someone may ask you, "Well, if you have faith, why did this happen to you?" Just ask Stephen. "If you are following God, how can He allow them to stone you?" That's God's prerogative. Why? Because He is the King and always acts for His glory. In the end, Stephen, graced with a vision of the glory of God and the living Christ standing at God's right hand, died with a smile on his face and a prayer of forgiveness on his lips.

Could you die with a smile as rocks were hitting you, and do so forgiving those who were killing you? Stephen did. His faith was stronger than rocks, and it was from his death that the Church multiplied. God used Stephen's death to give everyone else a purpose for living, including Paul, who witnessed the whole thing. If Stephen could die for his faith, can we not *live* for ours?

The Full Story

Preachers, Bible teachers, and other church leaders who talk only about the blessings, prosperity, and other good things that are part of Kingdom life are not telling the full story. Kingdom life is all of these and more, but it also is a life of challenge, trial, and hardship. It has been so from the beginning and will be so until Christ returns. How could it be otherwise when we stand as representatives of God's Kingdom in a world that is in rebellion against that Kingdom? The very fact that we are Kingdom citizens will bring us up against opposition and resistance.

Even in the earliest days of the Church, Paul and the other apostles of Christ found it necessary to continually encourage believers to stand true in the faith because temptations to abandon the faith were all around them. In the city of Lystra, Paul was stoned by angry Jews and left for dead for preaching Christ, but that did not stop him:

> Then some Jews came from Antioch and Iconium and won the crowd over. They stoned Paul and dragged him outside the city, thinking he was dead. But after the disciples had gathered around him, he got up and went back into the city. The next day he and Barnabas left for Derbe.

> They preached the good news in that city and won a large number of disciples. Then they returned to Lystra, Iconium and Antioch, strengthening the disciples and encouraging them to remain true to the faith. "We must go through many hardships to enter the kingdom of God," they said. Paul and Barnabas appointed elders for them in each church and, with prayer and fasting, committed them to the Lord, in whom they had put their trust (Acts 14:19-23).

Notice that after he was stoned Paul not only went *back* into the same city, but also visited Lystra again when he and his companion, Barnabas, made their return trip to Antioch where they had begun, strengthening and encouraging believers in towns along the way. And how did they encourage these believers? By telling them, "We must go through many hardships to enter the kingdom of God." Paul and Barnabas accepted trials, hardship, and difficulties as a natural part of their service as ambassadors of the Kingdom. It is no different with us. That is why we need a courageous faith.

Kingdom faith does not avoid challenges but accepts them as a vital and necessary part of faith life. Paul certainly understood this as well as anyone and better than most. An event in his life makes it abundantly clear that God often allows us to go through hardship for our good and His glory. Under arrest and on his way to Rome to appeal his case before Caesar, Paul was on board a ship that was caught in a bad storm on the Adriatic Sea. The storm was so fierce that eventually everyone, including the experienced sailors, despaired of hope. But then Paul received a word from the Lord:

> After the men had gone a long time without food, Paul stood up before them and said: "Men, you should have taken my advice not to sail from Crete; then you would have spared yourselves this damage and loss. But now I urge you to keep up your courage, because not one of you will be lost; only the ship will be destroyed. Last night an angel of the God whose I am and whom I serve stood beside me and said, 'Do not be afraid, Paul. You must stand trial before Caesar; and God has graciously given you the lives of all who sail with you.' So keep up your courage, men, for I have faith in God that it will happen just as He told me. Nevertheless, we must run aground on some island" (Acts 27:21-26).

God made it clear to Paul that it was His will for Paul to stand before Caesar where in the course of his defense, Paul would bear powerful witness to Christ. What is also clear is that it was God's purpose for Paul to endure the storm at sea and a shipwreck before he reached Rome. God could have made Paul's trip smooth sailing all the way, but He had a greater purpose in mind—that Paul's traveling companions as well as the soldiers and sailors on the ship should witness God's saving power in action and thus bring Him glory.

People of Kingdom faith do not avoid challenges because they know that challenges are a natural part of Kingdom life. Blessings, signs, and miracles, as wonderful as they are, make up only part of the picture.

Faith Outlasts Everything

It is for this reason that Kingdom citizens are known for the testing of their faith rather than for their blessings. Blessings are temporary; signs and wonders are temporary; but faith lasts forever. The saints listed in Hebrews chapter 11, the *"roll call of the faithful,"* were commended for their faith, not for their wealth or their education or their gifts or their talents. In fact, Hebrews 11:6 plainly states: *"Without faith it is impossible to please God, because anyone who comes to Him must believe that He exists and that He rewards those who earnestly seek Him."* Jesus asked, *"When the Son of Man comes, will He find **faith** on the earth?"* (Luke 18:8). Not blessings, or prosperity, but faith. Paul said, *"We walk by faith and not by sight"* (see 2 Cor. 5:7). In other words, we live according to our trust in God, not according to the things He does for us or for others—things we can see. Time after time in his letters Paul commended the faith of his readers:

> First, I thank my God through Jesus Christ for all of you, because your faith is being reported all over the world (Romans 1:8).

> We always thank God, the Father of our Lord Jesus Christ, when we pray for you, because we have heard

*of your faith in Christ Jesus and of the love you have
for all the saints—the faith and love that spring from
the hope that is stored up for you in heaven and that
you have already heard about in the word of truth,
the gospel that has come to you. All over the world
this gospel is bearing fruit and growing, just as it has
been doing among you since the day you heard it and
understood God's grace in all its truth*
(Colossians 1:3-6).

*We always thank God for all of you, mentioning you in
our prayers. We continually remember before our God
and Father your work produced by faith, your labor
prompted by love, and your endurance inspired by
hope in our Lord Jesus Christ*
(1 Thessalonians 1:2-3).

*We ought always to thank God for you, brothers, and
rightly so, because your faith is growing more and
more, and the love every one of you has for each other
is increasing. Therefore, among God's churches we
boast about your perseverance and faith in all the
persecutions and trials you are enduring*
(2 Thessalonians 1:3-4).

Why is faith so important? Because faith is the key to righteousness, which is the only way to see God or enter His Kingdom. As Paul reminded the Roman believers,

*I am not ashamed of the gospel, because it is the
power of God for the salvation of everyone who*

> *believes: first for the Jew, then for the Gentile. For in*
> *the gospel a righteousness from God is revealed, a*
> *righteousness that is by faith from first to last, just as it*
> *is written: "The righteous will live by faith"*
> (Romans 1:16-17).

Kingdom life is a life lived from beginning to end by faith. Faith permeates the mindset, speech, and behavior of Kingdom citizens. It shapes our view of the world and guides our decisions. Kingdom faith is resilient; it outlasts every weapon that comes against it.

Even when hope is gone, Kingdom faith remains. God promised Abraham a son in his old age, and Abraham believed God even after many years went by without fulfillment of the promise. He continued to believe even after he and his wife Sarah were far beyond child-bearing age. When human hope faded, only faith remained, but that was enough. In the words of Paul,

> *It was not through law that Abraham and his offspring*
> *received the promise that he would be heir of the*
> *world, but through the righteousness that comes by*
> *faith....*
>
> *Therefore, the promise comes by faith, so that it may*
> *be by grace and may be guaranteed to all Abraham's*
> *offspring—not only to those who are of the law but*
> *also to those who are of the faith of Abraham. He is the*
> *father of us all....*
>
> *Against all hope, Abraham in hope believed and so*
> *became the father of many nations, just as it had*
> *been said to him, "So shall your offspring be." Without*

weakening in his faith, he faced the fact that his body
was as good as dead—since he was about a hundred
years old—and that Sarah's womb was also dead.
Yet he did not waver through unbelief regarding the
promise of God, but was strengthened in his faith and
gave glory to God, being fully persuaded that God had
power to do what He had promised. This is why "it was
credited to him as righteousness"
(Romans 4:13,16,18-22).

When Abraham had no hope of a son and heir by natural means, he still had his faith, and by faith he received that which he would have gotten no other way. So if your situation appears hopeless, believe God. If you can't see any way forward out of the crisis you are in, trust in the Lord. Faith will see you through when your trust is in the One who cannot fail and who is always true to His promises.

Kingdom faith even outlasts death itself. Throughout the ages death had always been humanity's greatest enemy, an implacable foe that always won in the end. Then Christ came and changed everything. Through His resurrection from the dead, Christ broke the power of death and defeated it forever in the lives of all who trust in Him. Contemplation of this incredible truth moved Paul to write to the Corinthians:

For the perishable must clothe itself with the
imperishable, and the mortal with immortality. When
the perishable has been clothed with the imperishable,
and the mortal with immortality, then the saying that
is written will come true: "Death has been swallowed
up in victory."

*"Where, O death, is your victory? Where, O death, is
your sting?"*

*The sting of death is sin, and the power of sin is the
law. But thanks be to God! He gives us the victory
through our Lord Jesus Christ*
(1 Corinthians 15:53-57).

No matter what tests we face in life, even the test of death itself,
Kingdom faith will sustain us and give us the victory. When we have
faith, nothing can defeat us or separate us from our King and the
glorious riches of His Kingdom. Again, in Paul's words,

*Who shall separate us from the love of Christ?
Shall trouble or hardship or persecution or famine
or nakedness or danger or sword? As it is written:
"For Your sake we face death all day long; we are
considered as sheep to be slaughtered."*

*No, in all these things we are more than conquerors
through Him who loved us. For I am convinced that
neither death nor life, neither angels nor demons,
neither the present nor the future, nor any powers,
neither height nor depth, nor anything else in all
creation, will be able to separate us from the love of
God that is in Christ Jesus our Lord* (Romans 8:35-39).

Kingdom faith gives us courage because it assures us that we will
outlast whatever comes against us.

Faith Makes All Things Possible

In the Kingdom of God nothing is impossible because God has no limitations. He is all-knowing, all-powerful, and ever-present, and everything everywhere belongs to Him. It is this conviction of the limitlessness of God that fuels Kingdom faith with the courage to persevere in the belief that with faith all things are possible. Jesus was explicit on this point. One day Jesus encountered a father whose demon-possessed son Jesus' disciples had been unable to help, and he used the occasion to teach a lesson on the power of faith:

> *A man in the crowd answered, "Teacher, I brought you my son, who is possessed by a spirit that has robbed him of speech. Whenever it seizes him, it throws him to the ground. He foams at the mouth, gnashes his teeth and becomes rigid. I asked your disciples to drive out the spirit, but they could not."*
>
> *"O unbelieving generation," Jesus replied, "how long shall I stay with you? How long shall I put up with you? Bring the boy to me."*
>
> *So they brought him. When the spirit saw Jesus, it immediately threw the boy into a convulsion. He fell to the ground and rolled around, foaming at the mouth.*
>
> *Jesus asked the boy's father, "How long has he been like this?"*

"From childhood," he answered. "It has often thrown him into fire or water to kill him. But if you can do anything, take pity on us and help us."

" 'If you can'?" said Jesus. "Everything is possible for him who believes."

Immediately the boy's father exclaimed, "I do believe; help me overcome my unbelief!"

When Jesus saw that a crowd was running to the scene, he rebuked the evil spirit. "You deaf and mute spirit," he said, "I command you, come out of him and never enter him again."

The spirit shrieked, convulsed him violently and came out. The boy looked so much like a corpse that many said, "He's dead." But Jesus took him by the hand and lifted him to his feet, and he stood up (Mark 9:17-27).

How could Jesus be any plainer than when He said, "Everything is possible for him who believes"? This grieving father had faith, but he also was honest about his struggle with faith. He had suffered many years over his son's condition, and probably had sought healing through prayer and other means more than once. He saw a glimmer of hope in the news that Jesus' disciples had the same healing power as their Master, only to have his hopes dashed when they failed to cure his son. Now his faith was shaken, perhaps because he had placed it in what Jesus and the disciples could *do*, rather than in who Jesus was. When he met Jesus, however, this father humbly and honestly admitted his faith struggle, refocused his faith on Jesus Himself, and witnessed the impossible—his son was healed.

Kingdom faith wins because it looks beyond what is humanly possible—the limits of human understanding, achievement, and capability—and embraces the impossible, entrusting itself to the One in whom all things are possible. Because of its infinite scope, Kingdom faith is the source of exploits and vision that would be inconceivable on a purely human or physical plane. When Jesus' disciples asked Him why they had been unable to heal the demon-possessed boy, Jesus once again pointed to faith:

> *Then the disciples came to Jesus in private and asked, "Why couldn't we drive it out?"*
>
> *He replied, "Because you have so little faith. I tell you the truth, if you have faith as small as a mustard seed, you can say to this mountain, 'Move from here to there' and it will move. Nothing will be impossible for you"* (Matthew 17:19-21).

If mustard seed-sized faith can move a mountain, just imagine what larger faith could accomplish! Some of the greatest movements, ministries, and advancements in the Kingdom of God on earth began with the seed of an idea that was nurtured in the fertile soil of faith until it blossomed into full reality. Kingdom faith is not limited by what human vision, wisdom, or reason says is possible. Kingdom faith is limited only by the limitations of God—and He has none.

God never gives a vision or plants a dream without also making provision for its fulfillment. So if God has placed a vision in your spirit or a dream in your heart, don't deny it. Don't write it off as impossible no matter how remote or unlikely its fulfillment may appear under your current circumstances. Entrust your vision to the Lord. Spend your Kingdom currency—your seed faith—and trust your King to bring to pass the vision or dream He planted in you. It may take awhile—years, perhaps—but it will come about in God's perfect time. Remember, Abraham waited 25 years for Isaac. All the saints cited in Hebrews chapter 11 *died* without seeing the complete fulfillment of what they believed. This does not mean their faith was misplaced. It simply means that they placed their faith in One whose plans and purposes transcend both space and time.

The Crucial Choice

The message of the Kingdom of God confronts everyone who hears it with a crucial choice: believe and live, or disbelieve and die; believe and enter into a life full of richness and meaning, or disbelieve and descend into an existence without meaning or purpose; believe and overcome, or disbelieve and face defeat.

Judas Iscariot faced this choice. Even after betraying Jesus to His enemies, Judas could have repented. He could have renounced his betrayal, sought forgiveness, and renewed his faith in his Lord. Instead, he persisted in his unbelief, and despair over his lost faith drove him to suicide:

> *When Judas, who had betrayed Him, saw that Jesus was condemned, he was seized with remorse and returned the thirty silver coins to the chief priests and the elders. "I have sinned," he said, "for I have betrayed innocent blood."*
>
> *"What is that to us?" they replied. "That's your responsibility."*

So Judas threw the money into the temple and left.
Then he went away and hanged himself
(Matthew 27:3-5).

Judas' conscience led him to sorrow over betraying an innocent man who had called him friend but did not bring him to the place of embracing Christ as King of kings and Lord of lords. Judas' faith was misplaced. He trusted in his own vision of who Jesus should be and what He should do, and when that vision was not fulfilled, his faith never recovered. Judas' belief in Jesus never rose to the level of Kingdom faith. The tragedy of Judas' life shows us that when faith is lost, life has no meaning.

Simon Peter faced the same choice as Judas but with a different outcome. Having publicly denied Christ three times, Peter could easily have stayed in the downward spiral of denial and ended up dead like Judas. But he didn't. Peter's faith in Christ never wavered, but his courage did, and he failed the test not because he did not believe, but because he placed too much confidence in his own strength. Humbled by his failure (and wiser), Peter jumped at the chance to renew his relationship with his Master. There on the shore of the Sea of Galilee, the risen Christ gave Peter three opportunities to reaffirm his love for Him—one for each instance of denial. This time Peter passed the test, demonstrating that his faith was Kingdom faith: faith that lasts, faith that perseveres, faith that instills life with meaning and purpose. For the rest of his life Peter preached boldly, endured much hardship, and faced down opposition of all kinds with courage only Kingdom faith can bestow.

Like Judas and Peter, we each face the crucial choice in life: belief or disbelief. The key to overcoming in the tests and trials of life is to live by faith, which is the active, outward expression of our love for God. We demonstrate our love for God by obeying Him, and obedience is faith in action. Faith fueled by our love for God fills us with hope, the confident assurance of our eternal citizenship in the Kingdom of God. In the end, these three—faith, hope, and love—will remain when everything else has passed away:

> Love never fails. But where there are prophecies, they will cease; where there are tongues, they will be stilled; where there is knowledge, it will pass away. For we know in part and we prophesy in part, but when perfection comes, the imperfect disappears....And now these three remain: faith, hope and love. But the greatest of these is love (1 Corinthians 13:8-10,13).

This threefold combination of faith, hope, and love issues forth courage in our lives that guarantees our victory over the world:

> Everyone who believes that Jesus is the Christ is born of God, and everyone who loves the Father loves His child as well. This is how we know that we love the children of God: by loving God and carrying out His commands. This is love for God: to obey His commands. And His commands are not burdensome, for everyone born of God overcomes the world. This is the victory that has overcome the world, even our faith. Who is it that overcomes the world? Only he who believes that Jesus is the Son of God (1 John 5:1-5).

Why keep faith? Because it is the difference between success and failure, victory and defeat, peace and chaos, confidence and fear, courage and cowardice, and life and death.

Why keep faith? Because it is the currency of the Kingdom of God, and nothing transacts in the Kingdom without it.

Why keep faith? *Because faith guarantees there is life after the trial!*

Kingdom Principles

Courage is not the absence of fear. Courage is confidence and conviction in the face of fear. Courage is belief in life beyond the obstacle of fear.

Kingdom faith does not avoid challenges but accepts them as a vital and necessary part of faith life.

Kingdom faith gives us courage because it assures us that we will outlast whatever comes against us.

Kingdom faith is limited only by the limitations of God—and He has none.

God never gives a vision or plants a dream without also making provision for its fulfillment.

CHAPTER SEVEN

FAITH BEYOND THE TEST, PART 1

"Faith is putting all your eggs in God's basket, then counting your blessings before they hatch." —Ramona C. Carroll

Kingdom faith guarantees that there is life beyond the test. Faith, therefore, is the most important power we possess for successful living. Education isn't enough. A Ph.D. won't help much during times of stress. Book learning alone is of little use for a life that is falling apart. The only thing that can save us in the midst of turmoil and chaos is our faith.

Faith creates our confidence in life; our level of confidence is directly linked to the degree of faith we possess. Confidence is an attitude of positive approach. Remaining positive in the midst of a negative environment requires faith: the conviction that the negatives are only temporary and do not reflect the true picture. Only a person of faith can smile in the face of danger. Only a person of faith can be calm in the middle of a storm. Only a person of faith can maintain a good attitude in the midst of negativity.

Therefore, as we have already seen, our faith is manifested by the tests it encounters. In other words, testing reveals the quality and depth of our faith. Bragging about our faith impresses no one; our faith is proven in the midst of challenges. This is why God allows testing. Testing awakens our dormant faith so that it becomes active, manifesting itself in every area of our lives. We will never know how much faith we have or how strong it is until it is tested.

Our faith is only as strong as the tests it survives. And remember, God will not allow us to be tested beyond our ability to overcome (see 1 Cor. 10:13). This means that God controls the measure of tests. At the same time, however, we must be careful not to confuse the tests that God allows with the tests that we bring upon ourselves. James, the Lord's brother, explained the difference this way:

> Blessed is the man who perseveres under trial, because when he has stood the test, he will receive the crown of life that God has promised to those who love him.

> When tempted, no one should say, "God is tempting me." For God cannot be tempted by evil, nor does He tempt anyone; but each one is tempted when, by his own evil desire, he is dragged away and enticed. Then, after desire has conceived, it gives birth to sin; and sin, when it is full-grown, gives birth to death.

> Don't be deceived, my dear brothers. Every good and perfect gift is from above, coming down from the Father of the heavenly lights, who does not change like shifting shadows (James 1:12-17).

James makes a clear distinction between trials and temptations. In this case, trials are the common tests that come our way as part of life and that God allows for the proving and maturing of our faith. Temptations are the tests and troubles we bring on ourselves by our own sinful or foolish actions and decisions—the natural consequences of our inappropriate choices. Unchecked, these will bring destruction into our lives. They will result in deterioration, not growth.

So before you identify a challenge or difficulty in your life as a test from God, examine yourself to make sure you haven't created the problem yourself due to wrong behavior. If such is the case, confession and repentance is the proper course of action. Don't feel "noble" about bearing up under a trial you caused by your own sin. Humble yourself before God, confess your sin, and lay hold of His forgiveness.

Our ability to discern the source of the tests in our lives is critical to our ability to live successfully beyond the tests. Self-induced tests will tear us down while the tests God allows builds us up and strengthens our faith—if we allow them to.

Faith in Power, not Performance

Faith that works is faith rightly placed. In other words, the object of our faith—who or what we believe—makes all the difference between success or failure and life or death. Faith to live beyond the tests—Kingdom faith—is strengthened by conviction in the *power* of God, not His works. I've said this several times before, but it bears saying again because it is so important. Many believers today are so performance-oriented, so entertainment-focused, that the strength and continuity of their faith depends on regularly *seeing* God *do* something wonderful in their lives or the lives of people close to them. If God fails to act in some kind of tangible, visible manner, they become confused and doubtful, and their faith wavers.

The way to avoid this trap of self-deception and pseudo-faith is to make sure we put our trust not in the works of God but in the fact that God has the power—and the right—to do anything. Even if God doesn't always act the way we expect, we still must trust in Him and His power. God has both the power to do *and* the power *not* to do. He has the power to help or not to help, and sometimes we forget that. Our faith must be in God and His power because His power is more important than His works. Just because God's power is not at work in a visible, tangible way does not mean His power is not present.

Faith in God (not His power) activates His power. Jesus steadfastly refused demands that He perform a sign to "prove" who He was because such a demand revealed that true faith was not present. And where faith was lacking, little of God's power manifested. Matthew 13:58 says that when Jesus visited His hometown of Nazareth He *"did not do many miracles there because of their lack of faith."* Miracle power was present, but the unbelief of the people shut it down. Their lack of faith cut off their access to the miracle-working power of God.

So God has the power to act as well as the power not to act. Kingdom faith does not depend on *seeing* God act. Kingdom faith trusts in God whether He acts or not. *Kingdom faith believes in the midst of God's silence.*

Abraham is a perfect example. When Abraham was 75 years old, God promised him a son. He was 100 years old when Isaac was born. Abraham waited 25 years for the fulfillment of God's promise. How long would you be willing to wait? Abraham kept faith for 25 years because he trusted in the God who gave him the promise. He knew God's word was trustworthy, and God blessed him accordingly. Paul explained it this way:

Against all hope, Abraham in hope believed and so became the father of many nations, just as it had been said to him, "So shall your offspring be." Without weakening in his faith, he faced the fact that his body was as good as dead—since he was about a hundred years old—and that Sarah's womb was also dead. Yet he did not waver through unbelief regarding the promise of God, but was strengthened in his faith and gave glory to God, being fully persuaded that God had power to do what He had promised. This is why "it was credited to him as righteousness" (Romans 4:18-22).

No wonder Abraham is called the "father of faith." For 25 years he believed in a baby he never saw. Faith is what keeps us confident in the midst of the test. Abraham's faith never wavered regarding God's promise regardless of the length of time he had to wait. In fact, the longer Abraham waited, the stronger his faith became. What kept his faith alive? Abraham was "**fully persuaded** *that God had* **power** *to do what He had* **promised.**" He was convinced beyond doubt of God's power to back up His promise.

One of the greatest sources of our weakness as believers is our tendency to put our faith in the power *we* possess. Maybe that is why God sometimes reduces us to zero. Remember what happened to Peter. No sooner did he boast about his own "staying power" than he suffered a humiliating defeat. It wasn't until Peter was completely disabused of any confidence in himself that he could learn to anchor his faith fully in the Lord and find the power to stand up to any test. God promised Abraham a son. Abraham and Sarah were both old and far beyond child-bearing age. They had nothing with which to fulfill Abraham's need for an heir. It simply would not happen unless God kept His promise. So Abraham believed God without wavering—for 25 years—and saw the promise fulfilled.

For our own good, God will do whatever it takes to bring us to the place of total dependency upon Him. If necessary, He will reduce us to zero so that we will trust not in what we can come up with on our own, but in what He said He will do—and continue to trust Him no matter how long it takes for Him to do it.

Kingdom Faith Is Unstoppable

Once we begin to understand the true nature and power of Kingdom faith (or, rather, of the One in whom we place our faith), we come to realize that Kingdom faith is unstoppable. No power, philosophy, government, or trial of human origin can overcome those who trust in the Lord. Paul's eloquence in explaining this truth cannot be equaled:

> And we know that in all things God works for the good of those who love Him, who have been called according to His purpose. For those God foreknew He also predestined to be conformed to the likeness of His Son, that He might be the firstborn among many brothers. And those He predestined, He also called; those He called, He also justified; those He justified, He also glorified.
>
> What, then, shall we say in response to this? If God is for us, who can be against us? He who did not spare His own Son, but gave Him up for us all—how will He not also, along with Him, graciously give us all things? Who will bring any charge against those whom God

has chosen? It is God who justifies. Who is he that
condemns? Christ Jesus, who died—more than that,
who was raised to life—is at the right hand of God
and is also interceding for us. Who shall separate
us from the love of Christ? Shall trouble or hardship
or persecution or famine or nakedness or danger
or sword? As it is written: "For Your sake we face
death all day long; we are considered as sheep to be
slaughtered." No, in all these things we are more than
conquerors through Him who loved us
(Romans 8:28-37).

God has justified us through Christ. The word *justified* is a legal term. Remember, we are talking about a Kingdom and a government. Justification has to do with legal rights. To be justified by God means that He has given us our legal rights as His children and citizens of His Kingdom. He has given us what is rightfully ours through His grace. This being the case, Paul says, how should we respond? Then he asks a series of rhetorical questions.

"If God is for us, who can be against us?" No one. Kingdom faith is unstoppable.

"He who did not spare His own Son, but gave Him up for us all—how will He not also, along with Him, graciously give us all things?" He will. And what God gives, no man can take away. Kingdom faith is unstoppable.

"Who will bring any charge against those whom God has chosen?" No one. God has already justified us, and there is now no condemnation for those who are in Christ (see Rom. 8:1). Kingdom faith is unstoppable.

"Who is he that condemns?" No one. The only person who could is Jesus Christ, and He won't, because He died to save us from

condemnation. Instead of condemning us, He intercedes for us before His Father in Heaven. Kingdom faith is unstoppable.

"Who shall separate us from the love of Christ?" No one. His love is eternal and reaches to the farthest corners of creation and beyond. Kingdom faith is unstoppable.

"Shall trouble or hardship or persecution or famine or nakedness or danger or sword?" No. None of these things can separate us from the love of Christ. In fact, through faith, these things can draw us closer to Him. Kingdom faith is unstoppable.

With all of these things going for us, is it any wonder that Paul declares, *"In all these things we are more than conquerors through Him who loved us"*? Kingdom faith is unstoppable.

Nothing can separate us from the love of God, not even trials, hardship, or persecution. And since nothing can separate us from God's love, nothing can separate us from His power working in and through our lives. We may go through a few trials, a little hardship, or a period of persecution, but that is all part of God's process in bringing us to maturity.

Sometimes God allows us to go into hardship in order to bring other people out of hardship. Our challenge is to help them learn how to handle it. Paul and Silas endured a public whipping and imprisonment in Philippi for a night before God sent an earthquake to free them. As a result, many prisoners were set free, and the jailer and his family became believers in Christ. God allows us to go through tribulations so that when we come out the other side we bring a lot of other people with us. Kingdom faith is unstoppable.

Two Kinds of Faith

There are two kinds of faith in the Kingdom of God: faith *for* the promises, and faith *in* the midst of the trials. Both are legitimate forms of faith, but the second represents a deeper and more mature level of faith than the first. Faith for the promises defines the faith level of the majority of believers and Kingdom citizens. These are the people who love to serve God and believe God for what they can get out of it. While some may "believe" from a framework of self-serving hypocrisy, most are motivated by the desire to receive the blessings that God has promised for those who love and serve Him. At the basic level, there is nothing wrong with this, because God has indeed made many precious promises to His people and there is nothing wrong with desiring those. More mature faith, however, gets its motivation from a different place.

One of the main drawbacks to faith that is focused on God's promises is that it is very easy to slip into a mindset of expecting those promises to be fulfilled according to our preferred schedule, and most of us tend to get impatient very quickly. What happens if the promise doesn't come to pass in the time or manner we expect? Do we still have faith in God? Or do we throw our hands in the air in frustration and say, "Well, I guess faith doesn't work"? Our faith in God should never be conditional on the basis of the promises He has made to us. Promises are like the icing on the cake; they add extra sweetness to the wonderful things God has already done for us in Christ. Possessing God Himself is much better than possessing His blessings. Wouldn't you rather have the Source of all gifts rather than just the gifts? Wouldn't you rather know the Giver rather than satisfying yourself only with the gifts He gives?

The second, deeper kind of faith is faith *in* the trials, that is, faith that remains true *in the midst of* trials and hardships. This is the kind of faith we have been talking about throughout this book. Kingdom faith at its best and highest is always this kind of faith. It's one thing to believe as long as the promises are coming, but another to continue to believe when everything is falling apart. Anybody can have faith when he or she gets a bonus. Anybody can have faith when he or she has a steady job. Anybody can have faith when everything seems to be going his or her way. But what if you lose your job? What if office politics or favoritism denies you the promotion you are fully qualified for? What if your house burns down with everything in it? What if you lose a child in death due to disease or an accident?

These are the kinds of challenges life throws our way at times. Can you keep faith no matter what? Not if your faith is focused only on promises. You expect blessings, but disaster comes your way. You expect to advance into greater prosperity, but instead experience a sudden financial reversal. This is why we need faith that is bigger than faith for promises. We need faith that can handle trials; faith that can walk into a lion's den or a fiery furnace; faith that can handle a giant that is ten times bigger than we are; faith that can inspire a song in the middle of a prison. To live successfully beyond the tests requires faith that goes beyond looking for Christmas presents from Heaven all the time. It requires faith that will stand even when standing is tough and believe even when believing seems impossible. Faith that outlasts the tests is faith that says with Job, *"Though He slay me, yet will I hope in Him"* (Job 13:15a).

Faith Without Sight

Faith in the midst of trials means trusting God for the final outcome even when we cannot see the final outcome. As Paul wrote to the Corinthian believers, *"Therefore we are always confident and know that as long as we are at home in the body we are away from the Lord. We live by faith, not by sight"* (2 Cor. 5:6-7). We have to be confident in God even though we can't see everything. If we were in Heaven in the spirit world we could see the whole thing from beginning to end. But we are not; we are on earth in the middle of the thing, which means we cannot see the whole picture. So we must trust God who *does* see the whole picture. This requires us to walk by what we believe, not by what we see, all the while entrusting what we cannot see into the hands of Him who sees and knows all things. *Kingdom faith is believing that no condition is permanent or final but is under the ultimate jurisdiction of the King of the Kingdom.*

Let me explain it this way. Think about a rat trying to solve a maze in a laboratory. The rat is at one end of the maze, and a piece of cheese is at the other. Outside the maze is a scientist observing everything. The scientist is somewhat like God; he can see the entire maze at once and knows exactly what the rat needs to do to reach the cheese, every turn he has to make. The rat, however, can only see a small part of the maze at any one time. The path that is crystal clear to the observing scientist is a mystery to the rat. It must make its way through the maze gradually, step by step, discovering the next part of the path as it completes the current one. Only at the end when the rat reaches the cheese is the complete path known.

God is more than a scientist watching a rat in a maze. He is our loving Father saying to us, "I can see the whole picture, but you can't, so walk according to what I have revealed to you so far, and trust Me to show you where to go next." Living by faith means trusting God to get us through the trials even when our situation appears hopeless, trusting Him to make a way when no way seems possible. So don't panic when you can't understand. God understands, and He is in control. Do you want peace in the midst of your trials? Learn to say, "I don't know, but God knows."

Jesus said, *"Do not let your hearts be troubled. Trust in God; trust also in Me"* (John 14:1). Why? Because He sees the whole picture. Sometimes we are very close to a breakthrough but cannot see it because a wall is still in front of us. Only two more turns and we will be there, but that is where we give up. Ultimately, the only ones who will never make it will be those who quit before the end. Keep going, keep trusting the Lord, and you will get there. In the end, the race will go not to the swift or the strong but to those who refuse to quit, to those who keep going no matter what.

Paul's declaration that we live by faith and not by sight is another way of stating the wisdom of this proverb: *"Trust in the Lord with all your heart and lean not on your own understanding; in all your ways acknowledge Him, and He will make your paths straight"* (Prov. 3:5-6). Our understanding is limited, our vision incomplete. If we try to run the race of life on our own, we will end up falling into a ditch. The only way to remain in the race and to stay the course is to trust the Lord to show us the right path.

Part of walking by faith is opening ourselves up to self-examination, which is another kind of test. Successful people are always testing themselves, evaluating themselves, pitting themselves against new challenges and new levels to see how they will do. The only way to grow stronger is to exercise, stretching ourselves beyond where we have been before. It is no different with faith. Paul told the Corinthians, *"Examine yourselves to see whether you are in the faith; test yourselves. Do you not realize that Christ Jesus is in you—unless, of course, you fail the test?"* (2 Cor. 13:5). In other words, if you want to know whether you have faith, test yourself. If you want to determine the depth or strength of your faith, test yourself. See how much you can handle.

According to Paul, the way to know that Christ is in you is by the tests you survive. You always develop strength by heavier tests. The heavier the test you pass, the greater your strength. In effect, Paul is saying, "Go into life, pick up stuff that no one else is picking up, and test yourself to see if you can handle it. If you handle it, that's proof that Christ lives in you." This is the beauty of Kingdom life and faith. Kingdom faith is faith that is not afraid of tests. As a matter of fact, Kingdom faith is the kind of faith that causes the tests to come. It actually tests itself. This is why we should not fear tests and trials but welcome them as opportunities to grow, purify, and prove our faith. Every test we survive makes us a little bit stronger and brings us a little bit closer to the maturity God wants for us as His children who are destined to rule in His Kingdom.

Kingdom Faith Endures

Because Kingdom faith is anchored in the eternal God of unlimited power, it is unstoppable. This means that *Kingdom faith will endure forever, outlasting every trial and passing every test.* When considering the enduring nature of faith, we could find probably no better example in Scripture than the experience of Job. We've talked about him already in this book, but he bears returning to because his life presents such a powerful and encouraging lesson for us. How long would your faith endure? Could you go through what Job went through and still be standing on the other side?

Job was the wealthiest and most prosperous man of his day, rich in family, property, and possessions. He also was a man of faith who worshipped God continually. His troubles began because of a challenge issued in Heaven.

> *Then the Lord said to Satan, "Have you considered*
> *my servant Job? There is no one on earth like him; he*

is blameless and upright, a man who fears God and shuns evil."

"Does Job fear God for nothing?" Satan replied. "Have You not put a hedge around him and his household and everything he has? You have blessed the work of his hands, so that his flocks and herds are spread throughout the land. But stretch out Your hand and strike everything he has, and he will surely curse You to Your face."

The Lord said to Satan, "Very well, then, everything he has is in your hands, but on the man himself do not lay a finger."

Then Satan went out from the presence of the Lord (Job 1:8-12).

Through a rapid series of disasters satan took from Job both his wealth and his children, leaving him bereft of everything and destitute. How would you respond if you suddenly lost everything? Would you respond the way Job did? In the face of disaster Job proved his mettle; he showed what he was made of:

At this, Job got up and tore his robe and shaved his head. Then he fell to the ground in worship and said: "Naked I came from my mother's womb, and naked I will depart. The Lord gave and the Lord has taken away; may the name of the Lord be praised."

In all this, Job did not sin by charging God with wrongdoing (Job 1:20-22).

When faced with the greatest calamity of his life, Job didn't whine; he *worshiped!* In similar circumstances most of us would cry and complain and question God, confused by what was happening to us. After all, isn't God supposed to shower us with blessings and prosperity all the time? That is the mentality of many in the Church today because of some unbalanced teaching that tells us to expect only blessings from God and never hardship. This is not a new attitude; even Job's three friends assumed that his troubles were due to his sins. They could not accept the idea that a righteous God would send or allow such hardship to afflict one of His children.

Job demonstrated Kingdom faith, the faith that endures. He lost everything but still worshiped God because his faith was not in the things, but in the God who gave them. Job knew better than to put his faith in blessings because blessings are temporary. He understood that a house and a farm, that sheep, goats, and donkeys were all temporary; that even a family—wife and children—were temporary. Job knew that God owned everything, and that just as God had the right and authority to give, He also had the right and authority to take away. Everything Job had belonged to God, and God could give it or take it, however He chose.

Have you reached that place in your faith? Could your faith handle losing everything? If God allowed you to be stripped of everything you have, would you still worship Him? Would you still believe and follow God even if He never gave you another blessing on this earth? That's Kingdom faith, faith that endures, faith that changes everything. If your faith in God is based on what you have, then you will lose your faith if you lose what you have. Kingdom faith trusts completely in God and holds onto "things" with a light grip.

Notice too that Job did not blame God for his troubles. He *"did not sin by charging God with wrongdoing."* How often do we blame God when things go wrong? How many times have you blamed God for what's happening in your life? "Lord, why did You let this happen? What did I do to deserve this, Lord? Why are You doing this to me?" Our tendency to accuse God often stems from the fact that deep down inside we are not truly convinced that God really loves us or that He can be trusted. This is a doubt that is as old as Eden when satan succeeded in causing Adam and Eve to doubt God's goodness.

God is good all the time, and He loves us with an everlasting love. When we are convinced of this truth, we will never blame Him for anything that happens. Instead, we will trust in His love and goodness and look in faith to the working out of a greater purpose than we can see at the moment. Job did not condition his faith on what he had or on what he could see. Job conditioned his faith on the nature and character of God whom he knew to be righteous and just.

Faith No Matter What

Job passed his first faith test. Satan had insisted that Job served God only because of the blessings he received from God. When God allowed satan to take away Job's wealth and prosperity, Job continued to worship God anyway. Round one of the contest went to Job. So satan tried again.

> Then the Lord said to Satan, "Have you considered
> My servant Job? There is no one on earth like him; he
> is blameless and upright, a man who fears God and
> shuns evil. And he still maintains his integrity, though
> you incited Me against him to ruin him without any
> reason."

*"Skin for skin!" Satan replied. "A man will give all he
has for his own life. But stretch out Your hand and
strike his flesh and bones, and he will surely curse You
to Your face."*

*The Lord said to Satan, "Very well, then, he is in your
hands; but you must spare his life."*

*So Satan went out from the presence of the Lord and
afflicted Job with painful sores from the soles of his
feet to the top of his head. Then Job took a piece of
broken pottery and scraped himself with it as he sat
among the ashes.*

*His wife said to him, "Are you still holding on to your
integrity? Curse God and die!"*

*He replied, "You are talking like a foolish woman. Shall
we accept good from God, and not trouble?"*

In all this, Job did not sin in what he said (Job 2:3-10).

Satan contended that a man might maintain his integrity and
faith in God as long as calamity did not touch him personally and
physically—but touch his body with affliction, and he would drop his
faith like a hot rock. So God allowed satan to test Job a second time,
this time by attacking his health. Satan afflicted Job with oozing, pus-
filled sores from head to toe that not only left him in great pain and
misery, but also made him repulsive to look at. Yet even in this, Job
maintained his faith and integrity and refused to blame God. Even
when his wife, who obviously did not understand Kingdom faith, told

him to surrender his integrity and *"curse God and die,"* Job replied, *"Shall we accept good from God, and not trouble?"*

Shall we accept good from God, and not trouble? That is a key mindset for Kingdom faith. We have to be ready to accept bad things in life along with the good and continue to trust God either way. God allows tests in our lives not to break us but to prove us. He allows us to be tested—not because He wants to see us fail—but because He knows we have the faith to stand. But sometimes we don't know it, and we won't know it until we see it for ourselves during a time of testing.

As with Job, *people of Kingdom faith maintain their integrity even under testing.* Integrity means to be fully integrated; to be one with oneself; a unity, undivided in spirit, mind, and body. People of integrity say what they mean and mean what they say. Their behavior lines up with their words and is the same whether they are alone or with others. All their relationships and interactions with other people are characterized by transparency and honesty. Could all these things be said about you? Are you a fully integrated man or woman of faith who will believe God no matter what, who will trust Him in bad times as well as good, and who will serve Him even if you lose everything?

Kingdom faith doesn't fold under good or bad. Kingdom faith can handle good times and troubled times. Kingdom faith is stable. It doesn't matter what happens. Some people cannot survive success. Sometimes failure is good for us; it teaches us not to rely so heavily on our own wisdom, abilities, and resources. Failure teaches us humility and helps us see the need to trust God rather than ourselves. We dread failure because we think of it as a permanent condition. Failure is a temporary setback that can serve to develop our faith so that we can come out wiser than when we went in.

Kingdom faith doesn't ask for trouble, but doesn't shy away from it either. Kingdom faith faces trouble square in the face and stands no matter what, confident of victory because its confidence is in the God who cannot fail. Kingdom faith is faith that overcomes the world.

Kingdom Principles

Our ability to discern the source of the tests in our lives is critical to our ability to live successfully beyond the tests.

Faith to live beyond the tests—Kingdom faith—is strengthened by conviction in the power of God, not His works.

Faith in the trials means trusting God for the final outcome even when we cannot see the final outcome.

Kingdom faith believes that no condition is permanent or final but is under the ultimate jurisdiction of the King of the Kingdom.

Kingdom faith will endure forever, outlasting every trial and passing every test.

Consider Job's question: **"Shall we accept good from God, and not trouble?"**

People of Kingdom faith maintain their integrity even under testing.

CHAPTER EIGHT

FAITH BEYOND THE TEST, PART 2

"Faith makes things possible, not easy."
—Author Unknown

Faith is vital to life in the Kingdom of God, just as vital as food, water, and currency are for life on earth. We need food and water to sustain our physical life, and we need currency—money—in order to buy what we need. Remember that faith is the currency of God's Kingdom, and we cannot transact Kingdom business without it. This is why Scripture says, *"The righteous will live by faith"* (Rom. 1:17b). Kingdom faith—faith in Christ—is our spiritual food, water, and currency. After all, Jesus Christ is the *"Bread of life"* (John 6:35). He is the source of *"living water"* (John 7:38). Faith in Him (Kingdom currency) gives us unlimited access to the riches and resources of Heaven, because *"Everything is possible for him who believes"* (Mark 9:23b).

So are you rich, or are you poor? In any country, poor people are those who have little or no currency. They also have little power or influence because they lack the means to transact business. The more currency you have, the more you can do; greater is the influence you can have, and more significant is the difference you can make. This is why many wealthy people become philanthropists, endowing foundations and establishing charitable organizations. They feel a moral obligation to give something back to society, to use their money for good. Faith has this same value to our lives as Kingdom citizens. We cannot live in the Kingdom without faith any more than we can live in our earthly country without money.

How Good Is Your Currency?

Wealth is measured by the value of one's currency. If a government's currency loses its value, it doesn't matter how much of it anyone possesses. In the years immediately following World War I, the economy of Germany collapsed. The value of the German mark took a nosedive. Formerly affluent Germans suddenly found themselves penniless as the thousands or even millions of marks in their possession were not even worth the paper they were printed on. In our own day, something similar has been happening in the nation of Zimbabwe.

The source of our wealth determines the quality of our wealth. It is the same with faith. *The source of our faith determines the quality of our faith.* In other words, our faith is only as valuable as the dependability of its source. If our faith is in money, then our faith will last only as long as our money lasts. Some people have killed themselves after suffering a financial reversal. Loss of their money led to loss of faith, which led to loss of hope. Without hope, they felt life was not worth living. When the test came, they failed because they had anchored their faith in an undependable source.

What is the source of your faith? In whom or in what do you trust? Is your source dependable? Will it endure the tests of time and beyond? The quality of your faith is only as good as the quality of its source, so make sure you have the *right* source.

Faith always requires an object: something or someone to believe in. *The object of our faith determines the quantity, or size, of our faith.* The size of our faith can never exceed the size of its object. If we desire faith with unlimited potential, we need an object with unlimited capability in which (or whom) to place our faith. Currently we are in the midst of a worldwide economic recession. Millions of people have lost their homes, their jobs, their life savings. Businesses have downsized or declared bankruptcy. Banks have failed. Many homeowners with subprime mortgages have defaulted on their payments sending mortgage companies into deep financial crisis. A general mood of economic panic prevails at all levels of society. Why? Because the very thing most people assumed they could trust—the economic structure of society, including the stock market and the banking system—has proven to be not as dependable as they thought. If the foundation is shaken, anything resting on that foundation will be shaken. This is why we must anchor our faith in something that cannot be shaken.

Security is one of the basic common needs of all people. We all long for a sense of security in life, the confidence that we have built our life on something we can depend on. *Our faith is only as secure as the object of our faith.* Don't put your faith in a job; jobs can go away. Don't put your faith in a bank; banks can fail. Don't put your faith in government; governments can change. Don't put your faith in a pastor; he will disappoint you eventually in some way or another. Don't put your faith in signs, wonders, or miracles; they are temporary.

I learned a lesson many years ago that has carried me through many difficult situations: You can never be disappointed in what you didn't expect. King David the psalmist said, *"In you, O Lord, I put my trust; let me never be ashamed; deliver me in Your righteousness"* (Ps. 31:1 NKJV). David learned that the only reliable object of faith was the Lord God. People fail and things pass away; only God is eternal and unchanging. Although trust between people is vital for successful relationships, we should never place our ultimate trust in another person. God alone is worthy of our faith. Our faith is only as secure as the object of our faith. Put your faith in God and you will never be disappointed.

Similarly, *the stability of our faith is determined by the stability of its object.* In other words, if the object of our faith is stable, our faith will be stable; if the object is wobbly, our faith will be wobbly as well. And wobbly faith will collapse in the face of crisis. In recent months we have watched as millions of people worldwide who placed their trust in the supposedly rock-solid financial market have had their faith severely shaken. No institutions of humankind are dependable as the source or object of our faith. We must look beyond the natural to find stability. Jesus provided the best illustration of all regarding the importance of a stable foundation for building a stable faith that survives testing:

> *Why do you call me, "Lord, Lord," and do not do what I say? I will show you what he is like who comes to me and hears my words and puts them into practice. He is like a man building a house, who dug down deep and laid the foundation on rock. When a flood came, the torrent struck that house but could not shake it, because it was well built. But the one who hears my words and does not put them into practice is like a man who built a house on the ground without a foundation. The moment the torrent struck that house, it collapsed and its destruction was complete* (Luke 6:46-49).

The stability of our faith depends on the stability of its object, its foundation. Kingdom faith means that we dig "down deep" and lay the foundation of our faith on Christ, the "Rock." That way, when the storms of life and the torrents of trials assault us, we will stand as strong and as unshakeable as the Rock upon whom we are built.

*What is your faith **in**?* Upon what (or whom) have you built your faith? Have you established your faith on an unshakeable foundation? Jesus said, "*Have faith in God*" (Mark 11:22). God is absolutely trustworthy and thoroughly stable. He is the same yesterday, today, and forever (see Heb. 13:8). With Him there is no shadow of turning (see James 1:17). God is stable. God is solid. God is forever. And so are all who put their trust in Him.

An Unshakeable Kingdom

Nations come and go. Empires rise and fall. But the Kingdom of Heaven is eternal, ever present, ever stable, and absolutely unlimited in wealth and power. The only way we can escape the unstable and transitory nature of life in this world is to be linked by faith to God's unshakeable Kingdom. Scripture says,

> *For you have been born again, not of perishable seed,*
> *but of imperishable, through the living and enduring*
> *word of God. For, "All men are like grass, and all their*
> *glory is like the flowers of the field; the grass withers*
> *and the flowers fall, but the word of the Lord stands*
> *forever." And this is the word that was preached to you*
> (1 Peter 1:23-25).

This world and everything in it are perishable; they will one day pass away. But the Kingdom of God will remain. Kingdom faith has the same staying power because it is anchored in the King of creation who cannot be shaken. From that place of safety, security, and stability, not even the most taxing tests of life can dislodge us. On the contrary, trials and tests serve to strengthen and purify our belief. The strength and depth of our faith are proven by the tests we survive and the obstacles we overcome.

The turmoil in our world, whether war, economic downturn, moral decay, social unrest, political upheaval, or whatever, should not upset our spiritual balance or rob us of peace. We are merely witnessing the shaking of things that are only temporary anyway. Our hope—our certainty—is built on an unshakeable Kingdom. Knowledge of this truth should fill our hearts with joy and thanksgiving. As the writer of Hebrews puts it:

> *But you have come to Mount Zion, to the heavenly Jerusalem, the city of the living God. You have come to thousands upon thousands of angels in joyful assembly, to the church of the firstborn, whose names are written in heaven. You have come to God, the judge of all men, to the spirits of righteous men made perfect, to Jesus the mediator of a new covenant, and to the sprinkled blood that speaks a better word than the blood of Abel.*

> *See to it that you do not refuse Him who speaks. If they did not escape when they refused Him who warned them on earth, how much less will we, if we turn away from Him who warns us from heaven? At that time His voice shook the earth, but now He has promised, "Once more I will shake not only the earth but also the heavens." The words "once more" indicate the*

removing of what can be shaken—that is, created
things—so that what cannot be shaken may remain.

Therefore, since we are receiving a kingdom that
cannot be shaken, let us be thankful, and so worship
God acceptably with reverence and awe, for our "God
is a consuming fire" (Hebrews 12:22-29).

Anything created can be shaken so don't trust in it. Is your car a created thing? Is your house a created thing? What about your job? Your bank account? All of these are created things; therefore, you could lose them. God could shake them and take them away. Then what would you have left? God loves us and wants us to trust Him. In fact, He loves us so much that He will shake what we have if that is what is necessary to get us to stop trusting in ourselves or our possessions and instead to place our faith in what cannot be shaken. And the only thing that cannot be shaken is God.

As followers of Jesus Christ, we live in an unshakeable Kingdom. We are citizens of a realm that will never fall, never go bankrupt, never go through a depression, never experience famine, or poverty, or disease, or disaster, or setbacks of any kind. We experience these kinds of things while in this world because while here on earth we are living in foreign territory; our true home is elsewhere. The King is hard at work expanding His heavenly realm into the earthly sphere, reclaiming territory lost when satan usurped power from Adam and Eve in the Garden of Eden.

We are the King's ambassadors on this mission. Our hearts should be full of joy and thanksgiving when He blesses us with a little bit of Heaven on earth: personal stability in an unstable world and perfect peace while turmoil is all around us. But our peace and stability are not based on the things we have, which can blow away with the wind. We have peace and stability because our hearts are at rest *in Him* and no other.

Hebrews 12:28 says that we *are* receiving a Kingdom that cannot be shaken, not that we *will* receive it. It is ours right now. We are receiving a government, a lifestyle, a culture, an entire society that cannot be shaken. When we live as we are supposed to live— by unshakeable Kingdom faith—the rest of the world will take note and wonder how we can be so calm, so cool, and so confident in a world gone crazy. And they will want what we have. As I have said many, many times before, everybody is looking for the Kingdom; many people just don't realize it yet. They know they are looking for something, but don't know what it is. People all over the world are desperate for something to believe in, somewhere to put their trust, something that will bring peace, stability, balance, order, and meaning to their lives. Only the Kingdom of God can fill this need.

Kingdom faith is not afraid of anything because it is founded on that which can never fail or be defeated. People everywhere have been worn down by the world. Beaten up, broken down, battered by disease and disaster, torn apart by grief and loss, many of the world's people pass their days in lives that seem utterly hopeless. They long to believe in something that works, something that will bring them victory in life instead of defeat, something that will enable them to overcome the world. They need to see us, people of Kingdom faith, people whose faith will not fail no matter what we face. Then they will know that the Kingdom of God is real and that it works.

Trust in the Creator

The biggest problem with the religions and philosophies of man— their fatal weakness—is that they consider the natural world as the ultimate extent of reality. Throughout human history most people have followed religions that worship created things as gods—fish, birds, cats, bulls, trees, water, and just about anything else—rather than the Creator who made them. Kingdom faith, in contrast, worships the Creator, not His creations. This is in keeping with God's will and desire when He declared, *"You shall have no other gods before me. You shall not make for yourself an idol in the form of anything in heaven above or on the earth beneath or in the waters below. You shall not bow down to them or worship them"* (Exod. 20:3-5a).

We humans have an almost irresistible tendency to trust in the tangible—those things we can perceive with our senses, things we can see and touch. But appearances can be deceiving, and matters do not always turn out the way we expect. Wise King Solomon had this to say: *"I have seen something else under the sun: The race is not to the swift or the battle to the strong, nor does food come to the wise or wealth to the brilliant or favor to the learned; but time and chance happen to them all"* (Eccles. 9:11). While this may sound fatalistic, Solomon's point is that apart from God, nothing in this world is certain. And that is why we should never place our faith in the things of this world. King David certainly understood this, as evidenced by his words: *"Some trust in chariots and some in horses, but we trust in the name of the Lord our God"* (Ps. 20:7).

To understand David's perspective, we must travel back in time 3,000 years. In those days, any victorious general needed at least two things: horses and chariots. Why? Because they were key elements in one of the main modes of fighting. Foot soldiers were slow, but chariot troops could move quickly to flank or encircle the enemy. Without them, an army faced almost certain defeat. David was a brave and skilled warrior and the leader of warriors. He certainly understood the value of chariots and horses to his military strength. Yet he plainly stated that he did not trust in them, but in the Lord. David knew that his victories depended not on his military might and prowess, but on the Lord's favor. As long as he remained faithful, he could count on God to bring him victory.

Gideon learned the same truth. He defeated an entire army of Midianites with 300 men armed only with torches and clay jars. How did he do it? He trusted in God and followed God's instructions. It was the same with Moses and the Israelites at the Red Sea. With the pursuing Egyptian army behind them and the sea before them, they had no path of retreat and faced certain annihilation. Then Moses raised his staff over the waters, God parted the sea, and the Israelites crossed over on dry ground. When the Egyptians came after them, God brought the waters together again, and the Egyptians drowned in the sea. This just goes to show, as I said before, that no matter how hopeless matters seem, we never know the truth about the situation until we see it from God's perspective.

David said, "I don't trust in horses and chariots. My faith is in the God who made the horse. My faith is in the God who made the wood and the metal from which the chariots are constructed. Even if the chariots fail, I still have the God of the chariots." Is it any wonder that David won so many battles? David was the most successful king in the history of kings. The secret of his success was that he never trusted the soldiers or the swords, the horses or the chariots. Instead, he prayed to God and committed himself, his army, and the outcome of the battle into God's hands. Win or lose, he trusted God. It is because of this character quality of faith in David that the Bible describes him as a man after God's own heart.

Where is your faith? Put your faith in God. Don't trust in your spouse, boyfriend, girlfriend, family, business, job, school, or bank account. Whatever happens today or tomorrow or the next day doesn't matter; with God as your hope, you win—guaranteed. If God is for you, who can be against you?

Faith Through the Good and the Bad

Kingdom faith is belief in the big picture of God rather than in the daily details of life. Job's wife did not understand this. She had no clue as to the bigger picture from God's viewpoint. All she saw was that her once healthy and wealthy husband was now sick and destitute, and she concluded that faith doesn't work. This is why she told her husband to *"curse God and die."* In effect she was saying, "It's useless to follow God; look at where it got you. Why don't you just kill yourself and get it over with." Keep in mind that she was married to a man the Bible describes as the most righteous man in the whole land. She lived with a man who prayed every day, fasted, paid his tithes, and lived a blameless and upright life. Now, after losing their children and all their worldly wealth, Job was covered with painful sores and boils. For someone whose faith was limited to only what she could see with her eyes, it was only natural for her to conclude that serving God was pointless.

Job's answer is timeless: *"Shall we accept good from God, and not trouble?"* (Job 2:10b). That simple question reveals a world of insight about the sovereignty of God. God is God, no matter what. In good times or bad, God is God. Job's attitude was, "Once I was rich; now I am poor. Once I had much; now I have nothing. Once I was healthy; now I am sick. Everything I had the Lord gave me, and if He wants them back, He can have them. I love God with money or without. I will serve God with wealth or without. I will trust God in sickness or in health."

This is the essence of Kingdom faith. Kingdom faith inspires the heart to sing with complete conviction, "Through many dangers, toils, and snares I have already come; 'tis grace hath brought me safe thus far, and grace will lead me home." Faith enables us to go *through* the dangers, toils, and snares; faith empowers us to face either good or bad times with equal balance; faith ensures that God will give us the grace to endure all tests and come out shining brightly on the other side.

"Shall we accept good from God, and not trouble?" What a statement! But we have to define what "good" is. What is good from God's perspective may not be good from ours. It all depends on what serves God's greater purpose. "Good" may mean a fiery furnace as it did for Shadrach, Meshach, and Abednego. It may mean a lions' den as it did for Daniel. It may mean a cross as it did for Christ. It may mean a stoning as it did for Stephen. It may mean beatings, a shipwreck, imprisonment, and a martyr's death as it did for Paul. It may mean exile as it did for John on the island of Patmos. All of these things were "good" in God's eyes because they served His purpose. In each case of trial and hardship, He was glorified, lives were changed, and His Kingdom was advanced on earth.

Our God is bigger than any trouble we will ever face. Job loss? God is bigger. Financial reversal? God is bigger. A loved one addicted to drugs or alcohol? God is bigger. A child in prison? God is bigger. No rent money? God is bigger. Cancer? God is bigger. With Kingdom faith we can handle trouble because trouble is always temporary. No test will come our way that God will not equip us to face; there is no burden that He will not give us the grace to bear. The question we must answer: Do we trust Him? Do we trust in His unfailing love? Do we believe that everything He allows into our lives is for our good and His glory?

Job 2:10 says that throughout all his suffering and loss, Job *did not sin in what he said.* Some have accused Job of being negative. But in acknowledging that we receive bad in life as well as good, Job wasn't being negative; he was being honest. What's the difference? Honesty is accepting the reality of any situation even if it is unpleasant. Negativity is attacking God and blaming Him for everything that goes wrong. There is a tremendous amount of negativity in our world today and precious little honesty, even among believers. Like Job, we need to learn how to take good or bad, blessings or trouble, and accept them equally as part of God's program to bring us to strength and maturity. Our faith must be bigger than good or bad.

Some people cannot survive success. That is why God may reduce us to bankruptcy before He gives us plenty. And then if we forget Him, He may reduce us to bankruptcy again to remind us that we used to be bankrupt. God is more concerned with our character than He is with our coins. He can give us anything He wants, but He can't give us character. We have to develop character through tests and trials.

Rehearsing Our Faith

One way to build faith with character is to rehearse our faith. By this I mean taking the time to think through or "rehearse" how we would respond to God in the face of various worst-case scenarios. If your house burned down, how would you respond? If your spouse or one of your children died, how would you respond? Rehearsing our faith helps us evaluate the various elements of our lives in comparison to our relationship with God and discover that in the end nothing is more important than faith.

Job's faith survived severe testing because he had spent considerable time rehearsing it. Listen to what he said: *"What I feared has come upon me; what I dreaded has happened to me. I have no peace, no quietness; I have no rest, but only turmoil"* (Job 3:25-26). The disasters that befell Job are the very things he feared would happen one day. This means that he had considered the possibility more than once. He dreaded the thought of losing everything and going through suffering, but he acknowledged that it was possible, even for one who feared God. Then when the feared disaster came, it brought turmoil into his life, robbing him of peace and rest. Notice, however, that it did not rob him of his faith. This is because in rehearsing his faith—in considering worst-case scenarios—Job realized that in good or bad, in disaster or in blessing, in plenty or in want, God was still God and was worthy of worship. Job concluded that nothing that could happen in his life would warrant abandonment of his faith.

How often have you feared the worst? How much thought have you given to how you would respond to the arrival of tragedy in your life? Many believers who have been taught to expect only good, prosperity, and blessings in their lives with God are devastated when something bad happens. Sometimes their faith is shattered because they are unprepared for trials and hardships. Their lopsided faith has no room for it.

Pondering the possibility of severe trials and setbacks is neither negative nor unhealthy unless it progresses to a paralyzing and obsessive fear. Preparing ahead for trouble is a sign of maturity. In fact, a key operating principle for Kingdom faith could be: "Expect the best and prepare for the worst." This is a wise course of action, as Scripture attests: *"A prudent man sees danger and takes refuge, but the simple keep going and suffer for it"* (Prov. 22:3). Preparing for trouble today will help mitigate its effects tomorrow.

Rehearsing your faith means checking to make sure that your faith is in God rather than in the things He has given you, just in case the things are shaken. Do you believe in God only because He has blessed you? Do you define "blessings" only as the goodies, the promotions, the advancements, the prosperity...or does it also include the furnaces and the lions' dens?

God promised Abraham, "I will bless you with a son," but that blessing included a 25-year wait for a man who was already 75 years old. That may not sound like much of a blessing to us, raised as we are in a culture that demands everything right now. God's definition of blessing most often is not the same as ours, just as His thoughts are not our thoughts or our ways His ways (see Isa. 55:8). Abraham's blessing was not only his son Isaac. It was also 25 years of believing God for the promise—25 years of faith growing in maturity and depth. If Isaac had been born nine months after the promise, we would have nothing to learn from Abraham. What made Abraham the "father of faith" was 25 years of patient waiting for God's promise to be fulfilled. The blessing was the whole package: a 25-year wait, followed by a 9-month pregnancy, culminating in the birth of a miracle baby. And through it all, Abraham grew into a man of unshakeable faith.

Whatever you are going through right now is going to benefit other people who are observing you. Stand firm through your time of testing, and they will say, "You know, I've been watching you from a distance, and I can't believe how steady you have been through all of this. I know what you've been going through on your job. I know what they have been doing to you. I said to myself, 'He trusts in God; let's see how God works now.' I can't believe you remained steady all that time under such pressure! You've shown me that faith in God works. Teach me that faith."

And that becomes your witness.

Is your life in turmoil? Are trials and tribulations robbing you of peace and quiet and rest? God has not abandoned you. He may simply be shaking your life to see where your faith is, and, more importantly, so that *you* can see where your faith is. Can you have faith in the absence of peace? Can you remain stable when everything around you is shaking? You can, but only by examining your faith to make sure it is anchored in the right place: not in things, but in the Creator God who is King and Lord of all.

Kingdom faith is unconditional faith. It doesn't depend on what happens or what doesn't happen. It doesn't rise or fall on the basis of blessings or lack of blessings. Kingdom faith does not say, "God, I'll love You if You do this for me," or, "Lord, I'll serve You if You do that for me." No, Kingdom faith says, "Lord, I will love You and serve You no matter what." This was the attitude in Job's heart when he said, *"Though He slay me, yet will I trust in Him; I will surely defend my ways to His face. Indeed, this will turn out for my deliverance"* (Job 13:15-16a). Even in the midst of his troubles, Job's faith gave him hope of coming out triumphant on the other side. He also knew that faith was his *only* hope, which is why he said, "I will trust in the Lord, even if He kills me." In trusting God, Job had nothing to lose and everything to gain.

Job's steadfast faith paid off. He endured the tests and in the end, God blessed him with twice as much as he had before. And here we see another key principle of Kingdom faith: *Kingdom faith will always be rewarded.* It may take a while to see it—Abraham waited 25 years—but it will come. The reward may or may not be material in nature; God may not bless you with great wealth or material prosperity. But keep the faith; run the race; fight the good fight; and the Lord will establish your steps. He will guard your way and guide your path. He will lead you into a life of grace, power, meaning, and purpose, a life of fulfilled potential. By faith you will realize fully your destiny as a child of God and a citizen of His Kingdom.

Kingdom Principles

The source of our faith determines the quality of our faith.

The object of our faith determines the quantity, or size, of our faith.

Our faith is only as secure as the object of our faith.

The stability of our faith is determined by the stability of its object.

Kingdom faith is belief in the big picture of God rather than in the daily details of life.

Kingdom faith will always be rewarded.

CHAPTER NINE

THE POWER OF
KINGDOM FAITH

"Faith is believing in things when common sense tells you not to."
—George Seaton

Imagine that you are engaged to be married. The wedding is just a few weeks away. All the preparations have been made; everything has been bought; all the invitations have gone out. Your anticipation and excitement are at a fever pitch. And then, all of a sudden…your fiancée dies. What would you do? That's the kind of experience that makes a person want to quit, to give up on life, maybe even curse God. "Why did this happen to me, God? Why did You bring me this far only to leave me devastated?"

This is a true story actually. A man was engaged to be married to a lovely young woman. All the wedding preparations were in place, and everything was in order; they were simply waiting for the wedding day to arrive. Then in a matter of days, his fiancée suddenly took sick and died. The grieving groom went into severe depression. He even considered suicide. He felt ashamed. How was he going to face his friends and family? How could he emerge from such tragedy?

He almost didn't. His emotional depression became so severe that he was placed in an insane asylum where he received treatment. After a few weeks he began to come around, and after two months was released, having come back from the brink. He buried his sweetheart and went on with his life. Eventually he married and raised a family. But in that time of crisis as a young man, he almost quit; he almost committed suicide; he almost gave it all up.

That man went on to become the president of the United States. His name was Abraham Lincoln. Today he is still regarded as the greatest and most effective president in America's history. He shepherded the United States through a devastating civil war and held the nation together. He emancipated the slaves. Lincoln truly was a great man. Yet he could easily have ended his days in an insane asylum. Faith carried him through.

Another man less well-known than Lincoln, had a similar experience of loss. Just days before his own wedding, Joseph Scriven's fiancée drowned in a boating accident. Doubly tragic was the fact that this was the second time the young man had lost a fiancée to death days before they were to be married. From the depths of his grief and fortified by his faith, he wrote,

> What a friend we have in Jesus,
> All our sins and griefs to bear!
> What a privilege to carry
> Everything to God in prayer!
> O what peace we often forfeit,
> O what needless pain we bear,
> All because we do not carry
> Everything to God in prayer.

Have we trials and temptations?
Is there trouble anywhere?
We should never be discouraged;
Take it to the Lord in prayer.
Can we find a friend so faithful
Who will all our sorrows share?
Jesus knows our every weakness;
Take it to the Lord in prayer.

Are we weak and heavy laden,
Cumbered with a load of care?
Precious Savior, still our refuge;
Take it to the Lord in prayer.
Do thy friends despise, forsake thee?
Take it to the Lord in prayer.
In His arms He'll take and shield thee;
Thou wilt find a solace there.[1]

Joseph Scriven never did marry, but devoted his life to loving and serving the Lord who sustained him and brought him through such terrible pain.

Horatio G. Spafford was an American attorney who experienced tragedy upon tragedy. He lost almost all of his extensive real estate investments in the Great Chicago Fire of 1871. He decided to take his family on vacation to Europe, planning also to assist in the D.L. Moody evangelistic campaign that was going on in England at the time. In November 1873, Spafford, detained by urgent business, sent his wife and four daughters on ahead, planning to join them later. This was when the third tragedy hit. During the Atlantic crossing, their ship was struck by an English vessel and sank in 12 minutes. Spafford received a terse wire from his wife: "Saved alone." His wife survived, but their four precious daughters were among the 226 who drowned.

Later, as Spafford sorrowfully sailed east to be reunited with his wife in Wales, his ship passed over the approximate spot where his beloved daughters had died. Tragedy upon tragedy, yet being present at the place where he had lost his daughters inspired Spafford to write:

> When peace, like a river, attendeth my way,
> When sorrows like sea billows roll;
> Whatever my lot, Thou hast taught me to say,
> It is well, it is well with my soul.[2]

There is one common denominator that binds together all of these stories of tragedy: *the power of faith.*

Kingdom faith teaches us that there is life after tragedy, a future after failure. Consider Moses. Born a Hebrew; raised in the house of Pharaoh amidst great wealth, power, and splendor; educated by the most learned scholars in the land; Moses seemed to have everything going for him. Then he committed murder in defense of one of his fellow Hebrews and spent the next 40 years herding sheep in the desert. What a fall!

But what a comeback! God met Moses there in the desert and called him to the destiny that was his before the foundation of the world. Forty years in the Egyptian court had groomed Moses to walk in the highest circles of political power. Forty years in the desert taught him humility to listen to and obey God. Moses came out of the desert with a clear vision and a clear assignment from God to set His people free. Moses stood up to the most powerful king of his day and liberated over a million people from slavery. He became the inspired writer of the first five books of the Bible, from which come the fundamental principles that still shape the laws and governments of most of the Western world.

The Power of Kingdom Culture

Who among us hasn't wanted to quit at one time or another? We all have experienced times of disappointment or discouragement that left us feeling as though we could not go on. That is where Kingdom faith comes in. Kingdom faith assures us that there is life after failure. It gives us hope, the confident assurance that our trials and troubles are only temporary, and that a greater, fuller, infinite life lies ahead for us. It is this hope, fueled by our faith in Christ, that enables us to overcome the world. Kingdom faith makes it possible for us to remain true to Kingdom life and culture even in the midst of a worldly culture that is still largely under the sway of the powers of darkness.

We saw in Chapter Two that faith *is* the culture of the Kingdom of God. Culture is perhaps the most potent force in human society. Whoever controls the culture controls the people, except for those who make the deliberate choice to become countercultural. The power of culture leads us to several considerations.

First, *the greatest test of a nation is its ability to protect and preserve its culture.* Throughout history one of the consequences of conquest and colonization has been the erosion or transformation of indigenous cultures by the cultures of their conquerors. The Assyrian empire conquered the ten tribes that made up the northern kingdom of Israel, which had long since split with the house of David, the legitimate ruling dynasty in the southern kingdom of Judah. Assyrian culture completely consumed Israelite culture, and those ten northern tribes ceased to exist as distinct entities. A little over a century later, the Babylonians conquered the southern kingdom of Judah and took many of its people into exile in Babylon. In this case, however, thanks to Daniel, Shadrach, Meshach, Abednego, and other Jewish leaders who remained faithful to God, Jewish culture did not disappear. After 70 years, the Persians conquered Babylon, and a decree from the Persian King Cyrus allowed the Jewish exiles to return home. Persia subsequently was conquered by Greece, and then Greece by Rome.

In some cases a culture proves strong enough not only to survive through conquest but even to influence and transform the culture of the conquerors. Greece is a prime example. Although the Greek empire was conquered by Rome, Greek culture continued to flourish, deeply influencing cultures throughout the entire Roman world and beyond, an influence that is still felt today.

Sometimes a counterculture can be so strong as to transform the primary culture. This was the case with the early Christian church, which began as an illegal sect within the Roman Empire and advanced in size and influence to the point where the Roman Empire became "Christianized." The test of a culture's strength is its ability not only to protect and preserve itself, but also to transform a primary or competing culture.

This brings us to a second consideration: *the strength of a nation's culture is its ability to overcome countercultures.* In our own day, the pressure to overcome opposition is all around us. I believe that nations fail or succeed based on their capacity to overcome countercultures. Counterculture simply means a culture that gravitates against the primary culture in a society. Today the Bahamas, Jamaica, the United States, England, Canada, the Philippines, Haiti, the nations of Europe, and many other countries are caught up in cultural battles. One reason much of the Muslim world is in turmoil is because of violent protests against what many Muslims see as the encroachment of the corrupt "Christian" culture of the West upon the "pure" culture of Islam.

The early followers of Christ, the first citizens of the Kingdom of God, began as a counterculture within the Roman Empire. And even though "Kingdom Culture" which came to be known as "Christian" culture came eventually to dominate the Western world, the Church has always been at its strongest, most powerful, and most effective when it has operated in a countercultural relationship to the society in which it resides. One of the biggest problems in the Church today is the loss of much of its countercultural edge as many local church fellowships and individual believers have assimilated much of the mindset and methods of the primary secular culture, becoming in the process almost indistinguishable from the world.

This makes the third consideration of even greater significance: *the greatest test of culture is the social currents it survives.* Will the Church survive the social currents all around that are pressing it to compromise? We may not be able to stop other nations or cultures from doing what they do, but we can stop ourselves from doing the same. *Current* has to do with tide or pressure. Sometimes we call it peer pressure. How do we survive when everything around us is going against us? How do we successfully swim upstream? How do we emerge from the currents of social pressure with our integrity intact? It is impossible without faith.

And so we come to the fourth consideration: *the culture of the Kingdom of Heaven—faith—will overcome all the cultures of the earth.* The Bible makes this abundantly clear: "*The kingdom of the world has become the kingdom of our Lord and of His Christ, and He will reign forever and ever*" (Rev. 11:15b). The word *world* here refers to social and political systems. In this context it means the same as "culture." The Kingdom of God is a culture, not just a country. Heaven is the homeland, and earth is the colony. The Church is a Kingdom outpost charged with the mission of colonizing the earth for the Kingdom of God. Earth, therefore, is supposed to be filled with the culture of Heaven.

A Confident Kingdom

Culture is lifestyle. It is not a program or a project. Culture is the way people live. We don't practice culture. We are raised in culture so that living in accord with it comes naturally to us. Culture is natural; it's the way people are. Like any other nation, the Kingdom of Heaven has a culture, and one of the most distinctive characteristics of Kingdom culture is its absolute *confidence.* Kingdom culture will prevail over every other culture; it is inevitable. As Jesus said to His disciples, *"I have told you these things, so that in Me you may have peace. In this world you will have trouble. But take heart! I have overcome the world"* (John 16:33).

Jesus spoke these words the night before He was crucified. He was trying to prepare His disciples for the problems and challenges that lay ahead. First He gives them the bad news. "You're going to have a lot of difficulties in the world. You're going to face a lot of things that you didn't expect; a lot of things that you didn't ask for; a lot of things that you won't think you deserve. You're going to face some things that you never would have believed you would ever get involved in. You're going to face opposition, criticism, and attacks of all kinds. Things that you desperately try to hold together are going to fall apart. In this world you will have trouble. I am telling you these things in advance so that you will not be caught by surprise, but have peace when they come."

Then He gives them the good news. "But take heart!" That means, "Be encouraged; relax. Don't panic." Why? "Because I have overcome the world." In other words, "I have overcome the systems of power, the systems of culture, the systems of social currents, and the systems of moral values of human civilization."

Kingdom faith overcomes the world. With Kingdom faith you can overcome the insane asylum and rise to become president. You can overcome the pain and grief of great loss and be stronger on the other side. You can even come back from the desert after losing your dignity, character, and freedom, like Moses, and still become the deliverer of many people. With Kingdom faith you will make it because Kingdom faith overcomes the world.

A Powerful Kingdom

The Kingdom of Heaven is a Kingdom of power. It is strong and resilient. Many kingdoms of men have sought to destroy God's Kingdom and its citizens. Every one of them has failed. They always have and they always will. Trying to do away with the Kingdom of God is like trying to alter the very fabric of the universe. Creation itself is bound up in and regulated by the principles of God's Kingdom.

The Kingdom of Heaven is more durable than the kingdoms of the earth. Earthly kingdoms will all pass away, but God's Kingdom will stand forever. One of the characteristics of durability is patience. Patience can accomplish things that haste never dreamed of. A loser in life is actually a winner who lacked the patience to wait and to keep trying. Patience is a precious commodity, all too rare in our society these days. It is so precious that it is listed as one of the fruits of the Holy Spirit (see Gal. 5:22-23). I believe that patience is one of the greatest gifts God can give any of us. Proverbs 16:32 says, *"Better a patient man than a warrior, a man who controls his temper than one who takes a city."*

The virtue of patience is largely lost in our "got-to-have-it-now" world of instant gratification. Many newlywed couples think they are failures if they cannot immediately buy the kind of house their parents had to wait 30 years to afford. Many families today are buried under a mountain of debt because they could not wait until they could afford the standard of living they wanted. Insisting on having it all right now, they sold their financial freedom and made themselves slaves of credit.

The Kingdom of God is more durable than the world. Why is this important? As Kingdom citizens, we need to absorb the fact that we are part of a culture that never gives up. Throughout the Bible we are told to stand fast, run the race, fight the good fight, finish the course. Our problem is that we give up too easily. Many believers, particularly in the West, are not conditioned for hardship. At the first sign of trouble they throw in the towel. "Well, *that* didn't work. I guess it just isn't God's will. Let's try something else." Or someone at church hurts their feelings, so they stop coming. The preacher gets too "personal" in his preaching, and they're gone. They have no durability, no patience, no staying power.

Kingdom faith is more than "warm fuzzies," feel-good moments, and blessings. It includes all of these, but it also digs much deeper and demands much more. The call to Kingdom faith is a call to endure. It is a call to stand strong and never give up in the face of trouble, hardship, opposition, or fear. Kingdom citizens are part of a culture that can withstand any and all challenges, including death. Just ask the prophet Isaiah who tradition says was sawn in two. Just ask Stephen who forgave his murderers even as their stones were pummeling his body. Just ask Peter who again according to tradition was crucified upside down at his own request because he considered himself unworthy to die in the same manner as his Lord. Just ask Paul who was beheaded because of his allegiance to Christ. Just ask the countless multitudes of believers across two millennia who have suffered and died for their faith. If we could ask each of them, "Was it worth it?" they would reply in a thundering chorus, "Yes!" No price is too high for a Kingdom citizen to pay in the service of his or her King.

Since in Christ even death itself is no longer a fearsome thing, Kingdom citizens are not afraid of temporary trials, tests, and opposition. All trials are temporary. What we have to do is make sure that *we* are not temporary. Hurricanes move in with fearsome winds and destruction, but they also move out again. Whatever you're going through is moving, so don't panic—stand firm in your faith and let it pass on through. Our King calls us to stand fast and equips us to do so. Faith is the key that gives us access. Kingdom faith clothes us in the armor of God—and is *part* of that armor—that enables us to endure in the face of any foe or challenge, whether natural or supernatural. Paul breaks it down for us:

> Finally, be strong in the Lord and in His mighty power. Put on the full armor of God so that you can take your stand against the devil's schemes. For our struggle is not against flesh and blood, but against the rulers, against the authorities, against the powers of this dark world and against the spiritual forces of evil in the heavenly realms. Therefore put on the full armor of God, so that when the day of evil comes, you may be able to stand your ground, and after you have done everything, to stand. Stand firm then, with the belt of truth buckled around your waist, with the breastplate of righteousness in place, and with your feet fitted with the readiness that comes from the gospel of peace. In addition to all this, take up the shield of faith, with

> which you can extinguish all the flaming arrows of the
> evil one. Take the helmet of salvation and the sword
> of the Spirit, which is the word of God. And pray in the
> Spirit on all occasions with all kinds of prayers and
> requests. With this in mind, be alert and always keep
> on praying for all the saints (Ephesians 6:10-18).

Notice that Paul likens faith to a shield, a *defensive* weapon. If we never had battles to fight, we wouldn't need faith. Faith protects us in the midst of the battles. Your tests are temporary, so wait them out. In ten years your present opposition will be your friend, so don't worry about it; just pray. When I first met my wife, I didn't like her. But believe me, today I am *very* glad I didn't write her off then! You can never know what breakthroughs and blessings may lie ahead, so don't let temporary troubles now defeat you and cut you off from greater things to come.

The Value of Faith

One of the secrets of my stability in life is that I don't trust anybody. Some people might think that is a very negative attitude. It isn't. What I mean is that I don't put my ultimate trust in any human. If your life depends on what people think about you or how they treat you, then you might as well quit right now because they will love you today and hate you tomorrow. Today they will be here for you, but tomorrow they will let you down. The only way to stay steady is to keep faith in the Lord.

Remember, your faith is the most important power you possess, so as you run the race of life, keep your faith. As you anchor your life in God through faith, let your beliefs and convictions, which come from Him, create confidence in you for daily living. Then as you rise to face the tests and trials that come your way, your faith will be revealed and be plainly evident to others. They will see God's power at work in you and will glorify Him.

Your faith demands tests. As I said before, every faith confession will be tested. If you want smooth sailing in your life, don't go around bragging about your faith. If you don't want to be tested, keep your mouth shut. That's a fundamental law of the Kingdom. The only problem is you can't live with your mouth shut. So be careful what you say. Don't be like Peter, who boasted that he would never forsake the Lord, only to deny Him three times just a few hours later.

Jesus even warned Peter beforehand: *"Simon, Simon, Satan has asked [demanded] to sift [test] you as wheat. But I have prayed for you, Simon, that your faith may not fail. And when you have turned back, strengthen your brothers"* (Luke 22:31-32). Every faith confession will be tested. Peter boasted, and satan said, "Let me test that." The plain truth is that we cannot live Kingdom faith without talking about it, and whenever we talk about it, we set ourselves up to be tested. So we might as well get ready for it. How strong is your faith? You will find out when the tests come. In the meantime do everything you can to build your faith through prayer and the study of God's Word so that when the tests come, you will be able to stand.

Notice that Jesus told Peter, "When you have turned back, strengthen your brothers." None of us have the right to preach to anybody until we have survived some tests worthy of our faith. Many times the people who criticize the most are the very ones who are clueless about the situation because they have not walked that path. They have not been proven in the refining fires of testing. So before you criticize a brother or sister, ask yourself: "Have I been through what he's been through?" "Have I done what she's done?" How can you sit in judgment when you have not been through the test yourself? "After you have been tested," Jesus told Peter, "then you can talk about strengthening other people."

Criticism is a sign of immaturity. It stems from a false belief that we are better than another person. Never criticize a person whose history you don't know. You have no idea what scars they bear, what lessons they have learned, or what wisdom they carry in their hearts.

The testing of your faith is a sign that you are a Kingdom citizen. Testing matures us, but it also helps us learn discipline. And like any loving parent, our heavenly Father knows that discipline prepares us for success in life. The writer of Hebrews defines the connection between discipline and the growth of faith that overcomes:

> *In your struggle against sin, you have not yet resisted to the point of shedding your blood. And you have forgotten that word of encouragement that addresses you as sons: "My son, do not make light of the Lord's discipline, and do not lose heart when He rebukes you, because the Lord disciplines those He loves, and He punishes everyone He accepts as a son."*

> *Endure hardship as discipline; God is treating you as sons. For what son is not disciplined by his father? If you are not disciplined (and everyone undergoes discipline), then you are illegitimate children and not true sons. Moreover, we have all had human fathers who disciplined us and we respected them for it. How much more should we submit to the Father of our spirits and live! Our fathers disciplined us for a little while as they thought best; but God disciplines us for our good, that we may share in His holiness* (Hebrews 12:4-10).

Whenever you face hardship, take heart in the knowledge that it is evidence of your faith and of your Kingdom citizenship. By disciplining you, God is treating you as a son or daughter. His goal is to prepare you to *"share in His holiness."* In other words, He is shaping you to be like Him. This is just the way it should be, as Peter points out:

> *Dear friends, do not be surprised at the painful trial you are suffering, as though something strange were happening to you. But rejoice that you participate in the sufferings of Christ, so that you may be overjoyed when His glory is revealed. If you are insulted because of the name of Christ, you are blessed, for the Spirit of glory and of God rests on you....However, if you suffer as a Christian, do not be ashamed, but praise God that you bear that name* (1 Peter 4:12-14,16).

Peter tells us not to be surprised when "painful trials" come. Why not? Because trials are a normal part of Kingdom life and culture in this world. Trials will be absent in the life to come, but their presence in this life helps prepare us for the life to come. None of us who are part of the culture of Heaven should ever say, "I wonder why this is happening to me." We should never be surprised—or discouraged— when trials come. Some people may ask us, "If you believe in God, why is this happening to you?" Our response should be, "It's nothing. In fact, it's normal for us; it's part of our culture. It's just a passing thing. We are stronger than all of that." Wow, what a testimony to a world desperate for hope and answers!

That's Kingdom culture. We don't even waste our breath saying, "Why me?" because we know that our trials are building patience in our hearts and establishing discipline in our minds.

Many believers have the mistaken idea that trusting in Jesus will protect them from problems. That is a religious concept. If we claim to be Kingdom citizens, we must be prepared to prove it. Paul said that all who desire to live godly in Christ Jesus *will* suffer persecution; it's a given. Why? That's the way we prove that we are from another culture. Rather than fretting over our trials, Peter says, we should "rejoice" that we participate in the "sufferings of Christ." To paraphrase, we should rejoice in our trials because they prove that we are taking part in Kingdom culture. Jesus handled every problem. He suffered through everything and came out on top.

Peter says that we will overcome the world the same way Jesus did and with the same power. We will come through everything and will still be standing, steady, durable, and even stronger than when we started. In this way we will be *"overjoyed when His glory is revealed."* What is God's glory? It is His nature. God's nature will be revealed in us through the tests we endure. God does not want us to be quitters because quitting is foreign to His nature. Through faith in Him we can stay firm, solid, and committed while the world watches as the glory of His nature is revealed in us. If we are insulted because of the name of Christ, we should consider ourselves blessed. It proves that God's nature rests upon us.

Kingdom Principles

The greatest test of a nation is its ability to protect and preserve its culture.

The strength of a nation's culture is its ability to overcome countercultures.

The greatest test of culture is the social currents it survives.

The culture of the Kingdom of Heaven—faith—will overcome all the cultures of the earth.

The testing of our faith is a sign that we are Kingdom citizens; testing matures us, but it also helps us learn discipline.

CHAPTER TEN

FAITH THAT OVERCOMES THE WORLD

"Faith is taking the first step even when you don't see the whole staircase."
—Martin Luther King Jr.

The Kingdom of God is a fearless Kingdom. As we grow in our life of faith, we will develop a healthy degree of fearlessness with regard to both present circumstances and future potentialities. Where are you on the growth scale? Are you still struggling with faith issues, wrestling with fear, and having trouble trusting God even for day-to-day needs? Or have you matured to the point where you can honestly tell a friend or neighbor, "I'm not afraid anymore of what I'm facing"?

Ultimately for Kingdom citizens, it doesn't matter what's happening with the economy, layoffs, foreclosures, investment losses, property losses, business failures, fires, floods, natural disasters, and the like. As painful and difficult as they may be, they truly are insignificant in the eternal scheme of things. If you walk in faith as a Kingdom citizen, you will not fear or worry about these things because your faith does not reside in them; your life and welfare do not depend on them. You can face life and all its challenges without fear because your trust is in God who never changes, who cannot be shaken, and who reigns over an everlasting Kingdom.

So how do you get rid of fear? Open your heart fully to the love of God. Let His love fill you and overflow in you. God's love is perfect, and perfect love drives out fear (see 1 John 4:18). Another antidote for fear is the experience and confidence that come from persevering through tests. Every test you endure leaves you with one less thing to be afraid of. Once you survive a test, future tests in that area won't scare you anymore because now you know what you are made of.

How far has your faith been tested? Have you ever found yourself saying of a particular situation, "I never thought it would come down to this"? Well, get ready, because you haven't seen anything yet! Just when you think things can't possibly get any worse, they will. Just hang around a little longer, and you will see. But that still is no cause for fear, because faith will give you the strength to overcome any obstacle you face.

How far has your faith been tested? Most of us overestimate the magnitude of our trials. We tend to think that we are being sorely tested when really we are barely scratching the surface of suffering. The writer of Hebrews is describing most of us when he says, "*In your struggle against sin, you have not yet resisted to the point of shedding your blood*" (Heb. 12:4). In other words, most of us have no idea what true suffering is really like. God, in His grace, has spared us from it up to now.

Remember, God will not allow any of us to be tempted (tested) beyond our ability to resist. He apportions the tests according to our readiness. As our faith grows, so will the severity of the tests that God allows into our lives. In the end, however, Kingdom faith will prove stronger than death itself. This is why multitudes of believers through-out the ages have faced a martyr's death boldly, courageously, and even joyfully. They knew that not even death itself could destroy them.

The Kingdom Benefit of Trials

What benefits do we derive from going through trials? We have talked about quite a few in this book: hope, stability, maturity, confidence, discipline, wisdom, durability, perseverance, perspective (learning to see from God's point of view instead of our own), power, fearlessness, and discernment (distinguishing between the trivial and the truly important). Perhaps the greatest benefit of all is proving to ourselves and others the genuineness of our faith. This results in bringing glory to God. All of this is part of the complete salvation "package" we receive from God. Peter explains it this way:

> Praise be to the God and Father of our Lord Jesus
> Christ! In His great mercy He has given us new birth
> into a living hope through the resurrection of Jesus
> Christ from the dead, and into an inheritance that can
> never perish, spoil or fade—kept in heaven for you,
> who through faith are shielded by God's power until
> the coming of the salvation that is ready to be revealed
> in the last time. In this you greatly rejoice, though now
> for a little while you may have had to suffer grief in all
> kinds of trials. These have come so that your faith—of
> greater worth than gold, which perishes even though
> refined by fire—may be proved genuine and may
> result in praise, glory and honor when Jesus Christ is
> revealed. Though you have not seen Him, you love
> Him; and even though you do not see Him now, you
> believe in Him and are filled with an inexpressible and

glorious joy, for you are receiving the goal of your faith,
the salvation of your souls (1 Peter 1:3-9).

Through trials we come to a deeper faith, and therefore to a deeper understanding of what our salvation in Christ really means. Consider for a moment the benefits of salvation mentioned in this passage from Peter: a new birth; a living hope; an imperishable inheritance; protection by God's power; joy that transcends suffering; faith that is proven, and therefore valuable; a deepening love for God; and joyous assurance of God's love for us.

Once we realize all that is ours in Christ, it becomes easier to understand why Peter tells us to rejoice in our trials. Trials help prove the genuineness of our faith, which gives us an unshakeable conviction that all these benefits of salvation truly belong to us as Kingdom citizens. Our confidence grows during trials also when we remember that God only allows us to face tests that He knows we can handle. So we should look upon every test we face as a vote of confidence from God. The tests we encounter show how much God thinks of us.

The Importance of Genuine Faith

Proving the genuineness of our faith is extremely important because there are many so-called "believers" whose faith is false or who have confused or misguided conceptions of faith. False faith may talk big and sound like the real thing, but it will never survive the proving, refining fires of tribulation. Talk is cheap and often shallow. Faith *talk* must be backed up by a faith *walk*. Remember Paul's words, "*We live by faith, not by sight*" (2 Cor. 5:7). In a similar vein he wrote elsewhere, "*So I say, live by the Spirit, and you will not gratify the desires of the sinful nature*" (Gal. 5:16).

Kingdom faith rarely takes the easy path, because that is the way of the world. Jesus said,

> *Enter through the narrow gate. For wide is the gate*
> *and broad is the road that leads to destruction, and*
> *many enter through it. But small is the gate and*
> *narrow the road that leads to life, and only a few find it*
> (Matthew 7:13-14).

Many people assume faith to be nothing more than mental assent to a set of belief statements, but true faith is so much more. True faith not only affects the way we think and believe but also how we live and act. True faith transforms us from the inside out and *always* reveals itself in right speaking and right living. James put it like this:

> *What good is it, my brothers, if a man claims to have*
> *faith but has no deeds? Can such faith save him?*
> *Suppose a brother or sister is without clothes and daily*
> *food. If one of you says to him, "Go, I wish you well;*
> *keep warm and well fed," but does nothing about his*
> *physical needs, what good is it? In the same way, faith*
> *by itself, if it is not accompanied by action, is dead.*
>
> *But someone will say, "You have faith; I have deeds."*
>
> *Show me your faith without deeds, and I will show you*
> *my faith by what I do* (James 2:14-18).

True faith and action go together. Jesus said,

> *Watch out for false prophets. They come to you in*
> *sheep's clothing, but inwardly they are ferocious*

*wolves. By their fruit you will recognize them. Do
people pick grapes from thornbushes, or figs from
thistles? Likewise every good tree bears good fruit, but
a bad tree bears bad fruit. A good tree cannot bear bad
fruit, and a bad tree cannot bear good fruit. Every tree
that does not bear good fruit is cut down and thrown
into the fire. Thus, by their fruit you will recognize
them.*

*Not everyone who says to Me, "Lord, Lord," will enter
the kingdom of heaven, but only he who does the will
of My Father who is in heaven* (Matthew 7:15-21).

The tests and trials of life quickly weed out the false from the true
when it comes to faith. The false have no staying power. Jesus drew
this distinction clearly in His parable of the seeds and the sower:

*A farmer went out to sow his seed. As he was scattering
the seed, some fell along the path, and the birds came
and ate it up. Some fell on rocky places, where it did
not have much soil. It sprang up quickly, because the
soil was shallow. But when the sun came up, the plants
were scorched, and they withered because they had
no root. Other seed fell among thorns, which grew up
and choked the plants. Still other seed fell on good soil,
where it produced a crop—a hundred, sixty or thirty
times what was sown. He who has ears, let him hear...*

*Listen then to what the parable of the sower means:
When anyone hears the message about the kingdom
and does not understand it, the evil one comes and*

*snatches away what was sown in his heart. This is the
seed sown along the path. The one who received the
seed that fell on rocky places is the man who hears
the word and at once receives it with joy. But since he
has no root, he lasts only a short time. When trouble
or persecution comes because of the word, he quickly
falls away. The one who received the seed that fell
among the thorns is the man who hears the word, but
the worries of this life and the deceitfulness of wealth
choke it, making it unfruitful. But the one who received
the seed that fell on good soil is the man who hears
the word and understands it. He produces a crop,
yielding a hundred, sixty or thirty times what was
sown* (Matthew 13:3-9;18-23).

Look at all the "testing" words in this story: *rocky, scorched, choked, trouble, persecution, worries, deceitfulness of wealth.* These are the kinds of things that separate the true from the false. Many people have shallow faith with little root or depth. They seem fine for a while, as long as things go well. But the moment they hit a patch of rough water, their "faith" is exposed for what it really is: a shallow "bless me" mentality that is completely inadequate for handling the normal tests and challenges of life.

Then there are others who seek to use faith for their own purposes, such as the attainment of a worry-free life or the acquisition of wealth. When neither of these materializes, they quickly drop their faith and move on to something else. Only true faith holds out until the end—and enjoys the blessing and reward of an abundant harvest.

Plant your feet on solid ground. Anchor your faith in the Rock, Jesus Christ. Trust in Him alone because He will never fail you. As you stand firm in His strength, you will bring Him glory. People will praise God on your behalf when they see you go through tests. They'll say, "Wow! Your God made you strong. I thought you were going to lose it, but He brought you through!" They will see strength, not escapism. We should never be known by the trials we avoided. Your reputation should be built upon the trials that you came through. People will be impacted by God through the testimony you give, not by the things you never had.

Pseudo-faith fears failure because it sees failure as a sign of weakness, and false faith is all about appearances. Don't be afraid of failure. Don't get upset just because you didn't win. Sometimes losing is a good thing. It tests our resolve. And many times we learn as much or more from our mistakes and failures as from our successes. Be very wary of trusting anybody who has never lost anything.

For this reason, testing also is a prerequisite for leadership. Paul instructed Timothy to appoint no one as leaders in the church who had not been tested (see 1 Tim. 3:10). He was talking specifically about deacons, but the condition applies equally to all would-be leaders. Education is no guarantee of leadership ability. What matters is faith proven through testing. The last thing the Church needs is "hirelings" in leadership. Jesus said,

> I am the good shepherd. The good shepherd lays
> down his life for the sheep. The hired hand is not the
> shepherd who owns the sheep. So when he sees the
> wolf coming, he abandons the sheep and runs away.
> Then the wolf attacks the flock and scatters it. The
> man runs away because he is a hired hand and cares
> nothing for the sheep (John 10:11-13).

A hireling is someone hired to a position who has little or no personal or emotional interests invested. He hasn't been tested to see whether or not he has staying power. When trouble comes, a hireling abandons his post because he lacks any commitment beyond what is required for his paycheck. After all, there are always other jobs. Testing of faithful leaders will shape their discipline and character to shepherd the people with the same spirit as their Lord.

The Seven Roles of Kingdom Faith

As we approach the end of this study of Kingdom faith, I want to share seven key roles of Kingdom faith as it relates to us and our place in the Kingdom of God. While serving as a brief review of truths we have considered throughout this book, it will also reemphasize the indispensable nature of faith in Kingdom life.

1. *Kingdom faith is how we enter the Kingdom.* This faith does not come from within ourselves, but as a gift by the grace and love of God:

> *But because of His great love for us, God, who is rich in mercy, made us alive with Christ even when we were dead in transgressions—it is by grace you have been saved. And God raised us up with Christ and seated us with Him in the heavenly realms in Christ Jesus, in order that in the coming ages He might show the incomparable riches of His grace, expressed in His kindness to us in Christ Jesus. For it is by grace you have been saved, through faith—and this not from yourselves, it is the gift of God—not by works, so that no one can boast. For we are God's workmanship,*

created in Christ Jesus to do good works, which God
prepared in advance for us to do (Ephesians 2:4-10).

Without faith it is impossible to please God (see Heb. 11:6). This means that no one gets into the Kingdom of God without faith.

2. *Kingdom faith is our source of peace in the Kingdom.* Like faith itself, peace comes only as a gift from the Lord:

Peace I leave with you; My peace I give you. I do not
give to you as the world gives. Do not let your hearts
be troubled and do not be afraid (John 14:27).

I have told you these things, so that in Me you may
have peace. In this world you will have trouble. But
take heart! I have overcome the world (John 16:33).

Because the peace that Jesus gives does not come from the world, the world does not and cannot understand it. Christ's peace is much higher, deeper, richer, and fuller than any peace the world can imagine because it is a peace that finds its source in God. Outside of God there is no peace.

Do not be anxious about anything, but in everything,
by prayer and petition, with thanksgiving, present
your requests to God. And the peace of God, which
transcends all understanding, will guard your hearts
and your minds in Christ Jesus (Philippians 4:6-7).

3. *Kingdom faith is the currency of the Kingdom.* No Kingdom business is transacted without it.

According to your faith will it be done to you
(Matthew 9:29b).

> *And without faith it is impossible to please God,*
> *because anyone who comes to Him must believe that*
> *He exists and that He rewards those who earnestly*
> *seek Him* (Hebrews 11:6).

Faith currency gives us access to the riches and resources of the Kingdom:

> *Everything is possible for him who believes*
> (Mark 9:23b).

> *If you believe, you will receive whatever you ask for in*
> *prayer* (Matthew 21:22).

> *Therefore I tell you, whatever you ask for in prayer,*
> *believe that you have received it, and it will be yours*
> (Mark 11:24).

> *This is the confidence we have in approaching God:*
> *that if we ask anything according to His will, He hears*
> *us. And if we know that He hears us—whatever we*
> *ask—we know that we have what we asked of Him*
> (1 John 5:14-15).

We get things in the Kingdom by exchanging faith for them.

4. *Kingdom faith is the culture of the Kingdom.* The Kingdom of God lives and breathes by faith.

> *What does the Scripture say? "Abraham believed God,*
> *and it was credited to him as righteousness"*
> (Romans 4:3).

*For in the gospel a righteousness from God is revealed,
a righteousness that is by faith from first to last, just as
it is written: "The righteous will live by faith"*
(Romans 1:17).

We live by faith, not by sight (2 Corinthians 5:7).

*I have been crucified with Christ and I no longer live,
but Christ lives in me. The life I live in the body, I live
by faith in the Son of God, who loved me and gave
Himself for me* (Galatians 2:20).

*Clearly no one is justified before God by the law,
because, "The righteous will live by faith"*
(Galatians 3:11).

Any culture without faith is not Kingdom culture. Without faith there *is* no Kingdom culture.

5. *Kingdom faith is the evidence of the Kingdom*. The primary way the world sees and knows the reality of the Kingdom of God is through the faith of Kingdom citizens.

*You are the salt of the earth. But if the salt loses its
saltiness, how can it be made salty again? It is no
longer good for anything, except to be thrown out and
trampled by men.*

*You are the light of the world. A city on a hill cannot
be hidden. Neither do people light a lamp and put it
under a bowl. Instead they put it on its stand, and it
gives light to everyone in the house. In the same way,*

let your light shine before men, that they may see
your good deeds and praise your Father in heaven
(Matthew 5:13-16).

A new command I give you: Love one another. As I
have loved you, so you must love one another. By this
all men will know that you are My disciples, if you love
one another (John 13:34-35).

For God, who said, "Let light shine out of darkness,"
made His light shine in our hearts to give us the light of
the knowledge of the glory of God in the face of Christ.

But we have this treasure in jars of clay to show that
this all-surpassing power is from God and not from us
(2 Corinthians 4:6-7).

The faith and love we show toward God, as well as the love we show for our fellow believers, and indeed for all people, give clear evidence to the world that the Kingdom of God is real.

6. *Kingdom faith is the life of the Kingdom.* Only in the Kingdom of God do we find life—real life, abundant life, everlasting life—and we appropriate it by faith.

In the way of righteousness there is life; along that
path is immortality (Proverbs 12:28).

For God so loved the world that He gave His one and
only Son, that whoever believes in Him shall not perish
but have eternal life. For God did not send His Son
into the world to condemn the world, but to save the

world through Him. Whoever believes in Him is not condemned, but whoever does not believe stands condemned already because He has not believed in the name of God's one and only Son (John 3:16-18).

The mind of sinful man is death, but the mind controlled by the Spirit is life and peace (Romans 8:6).

Faith is the very lifeblood of every Kingdom citizen.

7. *Kingdom faith creates the environment of the Kingdom.* A faith-filled environment can work miracles. When faith is present, lives are transformed, which is the greatest miracle of all.

Just then a woman who had been subject to bleeding for twelve years came up behind Him and touched the edge of His cloak. She said to herself, "If I only touch His cloak, I will be healed."

Jesus turned and saw her. "Take heart, daughter," He said, "your faith has healed you." And the woman was healed from that moment (Matthew 9:20-22).

Then Jesus answered, "Woman, you have great faith! Your request is granted." And her daughter was healed from that very hour (Matthew 15:28).

"What do you want Me to do for you?" Jesus asked him.

The blind man said, "Rabbi, I want to see."

"Go," said Jesus, "your faith has healed you."
Immediately he received his sight and followed Jesus
along the road (Mark 10:51-52).

In Lystra there sat a man crippled in his feet, who was
lame from birth and had never walked. He listened to
Paul as he was speaking. Paul looked directly at him,
saw that he had faith to be healed and called out,
"Stand up on your feet!" At that, the man jumped up
and began to walk (Acts 14:8-10).

Faith comes by hearing, and hearing by the Word of God (see Rom. 10:17). Our belief rises under the environment of faith, which is how we become active citizens in the Kingdom of God. We don't get things from God just because we *claim* we believe God; we get things from God because we *believe* God. The difference often hinges on the presence or absence of tests. We don't truly come to know and believe God until we go through a living hell. It is when we are stripped of all our own resources, when we are at the end of our rope, that we discover the all-sufficiency of God.

Faith That Overcomes the World

As long as you have faith, you are still in the game of life. And you don't have to have a lot of faith, but your faith has to be real. Even the tiniest bit of genuine faith can do unbelievable things:

The apostles said to the Lord, "Increase our faith!"

He replied, "If you have faith as small as a mustard
seed, you can say to this mulberry tree, 'Be uprooted

and planted in the sea,' and it will obey you"
(Luke 17:5-6).

*"Have faith in God," Jesus answered. "I tell you the
truth, if anyone says to this mountain, 'Go, throw
yourself into the sea,' and does not doubt in his heart
but believes that what he says will happen, it will be
done for him. Therefore I tell you, whatever you ask for
in prayer, believe that you have received it, and it will
be yours"* (Mark 11:22-24).

Have you seen any trees or mountains uprooted and thrown into
the sea lately? No? What does that say about the quality of our faith?
As these verses indicate, the *size* of our faith isn't the issue, the *presence* of it is! Just the tiniest grain of genuine, unreserved, no-holds-barred faith in God is all it takes to move a mountain, whether it is
a mountain of ill health, a mountain of financial hardship, a mountain of criticism and opposition, or a mountain of unemployment.
Whatever your mountain, all you need to move it is a grain of pure
faith, the tiniest penny of Kingdom currency. Can you see now why
the Bible says that our faith will overcome the world?

Listen to the voice of God. He is saying, "The size of your mountain isn't the issue. The magnitude of the tests you face isn't the issue.
The issue is this: do you believe Me?"

If you can honestly answer "Yes" to that question, then get ready
to see mountains moved in your life as never before. It may not be
today or tomorrow or even a year from now, but "moving day" will
come. In God's own time and way, it will come. Kingdom faith overcomes the world—*guaranteed!*

For everyone born of God overcomes the world. This is the victory that has overcome the world, even our faith. Who is it that overcomes the world? Only he who believes that Jesus is the Son of God (1 John 5:4-5).

Kingdom Principles

Kingdom faith is how we enter the Kingdom.

Kingdom faith is our source of peace in the Kingdom.

Kingdom faith is the currency of the Kingdom.

Kingdom faith is the culture of the Kingdom.

Kingdom faith is the evidence of the Kingdom.

Kingdom faith is the life of the Kingdom.

Kingdom faith creates the environment of the Kingdom.

Kingdom faith overcomes the world—guaranteed!

CONCLUSION

Life will always be filled with mysteries and questions we cannot answer. We will always face tests, circumstances, and situations that challenge the very core of our confidence and stability. There will be times when we will encounter moments of fear, despair, hopelessness, and confusion that will give birth to doubt that renders us helpless and immobilized. Life will bring us the unexpected and the unbelievable, sending shock waves through our traditional convictions and causing us to wonder if there really is a loving Creator who cares about our plight.

Life will many times hit us from the blind side with obstacles and pressures that have no pattern. In essence, for each of us, life is an earthly journey that does not come with a map. I have come to the conclusion that we were created to live by trust and explore the unknown with the compass of faith. To live effectively on this earth we must accept the fact that we will face opportunities to doubt and that everything we believe will be challenged. This is the nature of life, and if you live on the planet, tests and trials will be common and normal.

If you accept the reality of trials and tests as the nature of life on earth, then you will be neither disappointed nor overwhelmed when they arrive. In fact, the best weapon against trials is to see them as tools in the hands of a skillful Sculptor dedicated to the task of unveiling from the block of your existence a perfected image of the real you. I challenge you to trust the divine Sculptor and have faith in His vision of who you really are. May you live a life that embraces the spirit of the words of the great first-century apostle James who declared,

> Consider it pure joy, my brothers, whenever you
> face trials of many kinds, because you know that
> the testing of your faith develops perseverance.
> Perseverance must finish its work so that you may be
> mature and complete, not lacking anything
> (James 1:2-4).

> Blessed is the man who perseveres under trial, because
> when he has stood the test, he will receive the crown
> of life that God has promised to those who love Him
> (James 1:12).

Be inspired by the words of the great patriarch of the church, Peter, who reiterates the same sentiments in his statement: "*In this you greatly rejoice, though now for a little while you may have had to suffer grief in all kinds of trials. These have come so that your faith—of greater worth than gold, which perishes even though refined by fire— may be proved genuine and may result in praise, glory and honor when Jesus Christ is revealed*" (1 Pet. 1:6-7).

The beloved apostle John further injects this spirit of faith, giving you and me the secret to overcoming every obstacle in life: "*And His commands are not burdensome, for everyone born of God overcomes the world. This is the victory that has overcome the world, even our faith"* (1 John 5:3-4).

The writer of the Book of Hebrews sums it all up in these words:

> *But My righteous one will live by faith. And if he shrinks back, I will not be pleased with him* (Hebrews 10:38).

> *And without faith it is impossible to please God, because anyone who comes to Him must believe that He exists and that He rewards those who earnestly seek Him* (Hebrews 11:6).

So I challenge you to be a faith-filled Kingdom citizen. May you rise to every occasion and face the future with a confidence that intimidates trials and embarrasses the skeptics, knowing that nothing can stop the power of your belief. May you live by this motto: "When in doubt...have faith." Be always mindful that you have the image and nature of your Creator, a nature that is fearless, bold, and stronger than death and life. As long as you believe, you win. Protect your capacity to believe knowing that everything except your destiny is temporary. Doubt is not an option, and faith is a necessity. Live and walk daily by Kingdom faith, and I will see you on the other side of your trials.

Myles Munroe International

The Diplomat Center

P.O. Box N-9583

Nassau, Bahamas

Tel: 242-461-6423

Website: www.mylesmunroeinternational.com
Email: mmi@mylesmunroeinternational.com

THE ISLANDS OF THE
bahamas

For Information on Bahamas Religious Tourism

Tel: 1-800-224-3681

Website: worship.bahamas.com

Additional copies of this book and other
book titles from Destiny Image are
available at your local bookstore.

Call toll-free: 1-800-722-6774.

Send a request for a catalog to:

Destiny Image® Publishers, Inc.
P.O. Box 310
Shippensburg, PA 17257-0310

*"Speaking to the Purposes of God for This
Generation and for the Generations to Come."*

**For a complete list of our titles,
visit us at www.destinyimage.com.**